INSIDE CONGRESS

INSIDE CONGRESS

A Guide for Navigating the Politics
of the House and Senate Floors

Trevor Corning

Reema Dodin

Kyle Nevins

The Brookings Institution is a private nonprofit organization devoted to research, education, and publication on important issues of domestic and foreign policy. Its principal purpose is to bring the highest quality independent research and analysis to bear on current and emerging policy problems. Interpretations or conclusions in Brookings publications should be understood to be solely those of the authors.

Library of Congress Cataloging-in-Publication data

Names: Corning, Trevor, author. | Dodin, Reema, author. | Nevins, Kyle W., author.
Title: Inside Congress : a guide for navigating the politics of the House and Senate floors / Trevor Corning, Reema Dodin, Kyle W. Nevins.
Description: Washington, D.C. : Brookings Institution Press, 2017.
Identifiers: LCCN 2016045229 (print) | LCCN 2016057111 (ebook) | ISBN 9780815727323 (paperback) | ISBN 9780815727347 (epub) | ISBN 9780815727354 (pdf)
Subjects: LCSH: United States. Congress. | Legislation—United States. | BISAC: POLITICAL SCIENCE / Government / Legislative Branch. | POLITICAL SCIENCE / Government / National. | POLITICAL SCIENCE / Political Process / Political Parties.
Classification: LCC JK1021 .C68 2017 (print) | LCC JK1021 (ebook) | DDC 325.73—dc23
LC record available at https://lccn.loc.gov/2016045229

9 8 7 6 5 4 3 2

Typeset in Caslon

Composition by Westchester Publishing Services

Contents

Acknowledgments

Special thanks to
Our families and loved ones for supporting us along the way.
Washington University in St. Louis
Marty Paone
Tom Wickham
Hon. Robert M. Carr

ONE

Introduction and Overview
Two Chambers, Two Ways

All legislative Powers herein granted shall be vested in a Congress of the United States, which shall consist of a Senate and House of Representatives.
> —*U.S. Constitution, Article 1, Section 1*

The Congress shall have Power To lay and collect Taxes, Duties, Imposts and Excises, to pay the Debts and provide for the common Defence and general Welfare of the United States; but all Duties, Imposts and Excises shall be uniform throughout the United States; . . . To make all Laws which shall be necessary and proper for carrying into Execution the foregoing Powers, and all other Powers vested by this Constitution in the Government of the United States, or in any Department or Officer thereof.
> *U.S. Constitution, Article 1, Section 8*

The first article of the United States Constitution vests law-making powers in the U.S. Congress and specifies that it is a bicameral, or two-chamber, legislature, with a Senate and a House of Representatives. Both chambers are located in the Capitol Building, in Washington, D.C. The two chambers of Congress reflect the both competing and complimentary ideas of elected officials— closely representative and responsive to their constituents, as it is for House members, and heavily considerate of divergent ideas across large groups of voters, as it is for senators.

This basic difference in the makeup of the two houses of Congress determined other decisions the Framers made, such as the terms of office of representatives versus senators, the timing of elections, and many of the specific duties of each house of Congress. All of this is set forth in the first two articles of the Constitution. Despite some changes over the centuries—probably the most significant being that senators are now elected via a popular vote within their respective states—these distinctions have been reflected in the two chambers of Congress to the present day.

For each chamber the Constitution specifies certain duties and privileges. In addition, Article 1, Section 5, states, "Each House may determine the Rules of its Proceedings"—how they will actually do the work of making the laws of the land. The rules of each chamber have greatly evolved since the 1st Congress met, in ways that reflect the systemic and cultural differences of the two distinct bodies, and American history itself. As the business of the Congress evolved over the centuries, the rules the chambers made for themselves became more expansive. This complexity can cause confusion for those interacting with Congress and for those watching from afar and trying to understand the proceedings. Often the difficulty in working with Congress stems from a misunderstanding of why rules or procedures matter and how they are used.

A great deal has been written about Congress and its members, much of it complicated, procedural, or just plainly subjective. We aim to set forth in this volume a nonpartisan, straightforward view of the machinery that drives each of the two chambers of the American legislative branch. We hope that the terms, definitions, and explanations that follow give readers tools to help them understand why Congress operates as it does as they follow legislative ups and downs through television coverage, news articles, op-eds, or CSPAN. And that readers' own critical views, now better informed as to what is going on, will make them more effective congressional watchers, staffers, or advocates.

We write with two overarching themes in mind. The first is that the two chambers are fundamentally different. The chambers differ markedly in the types of pressures on their members, the way they are run, and the ways their respective leaderships operate. All House members must stand for election every two years, and every two years a new House is formed. This shorter time frame means that representatives must keep their fingers on the pulse of their districts and even of their individual constituents. This shorter electoral horizon is meant to reflect the passions of the people.

Senators, by contrast, face reelection every six years, and challengers to a Senate seat have fewer chances and must wait longer to try to upset the status quo. In the Senate, change occurs more slowly. Members have longer to get to know one another and to work together than is the case in the House. That is why the Senate traditionally has been called the cooling saucer, where members have time to consider issues and are insulated from the passions of the moment. Yet there is great debate as to whether this remains the case in the modern Senate.

The size of the bodies also affects the rules and procedures in the two chambers to move legislation forward. The need to manage 435 representatives contributes to why the House is more clearly majoritarian ruled, in that the majority party calls the shots, and members often yield to the majority will. The Senate is more likely to accommodate the wishes of individual senators, and all 100 senators have extensive tools at their disposal to shape debate on the Senate floor. The Senate also provides the greatest continuity. Whereas the House changes every two years, and the president may change every four years, in the Senate two-thirds remains the same after any given election because only one-third of its members are up for election in each two-year election period.

The second overarching theme is that although the procedures of both chambers are relatively complicated, and the documents explaining them perhaps a bit cumbersome, on any given day the House and Senate are likely to use only a fraction of the procedures or maneuvers available. In other words, most of Congress's business is covered by a small number of the tools available. We do not cover every possible move and maneuver that an individual or a group of legislators might use here— and if you watch the floors long enough you will see some interesting and unusual things. Instead, we aim to explain to readers the main tools they need to understand in order to be informed watchers of the House and Senate—to read the tea leaves of what is happening on each floor and understand the context well enough to follow along as each chamber goes about its floor work. Once you have a good understanding of the basics, texts that cover all of the possible maneuvers—including those rarely used—may make more sense.

Congress, as the legislative branch of government, has constitutional powers and duties that it must fulfill that are not all equally applied to each chamber (such as the Senate has duties of advise and consent for nominations). This, plus their structural differences, lead the House and Senate to often function independently on pieces of legislation. Ultimately, they must act in concert legislatively to fulfill their constitutional obligations, such as managing the financial balance sheet of the nation and making laws to maintain the functions of the U.S. government.

Inside Congress is a brief work intended to empower you, the reader—regardless of whether you are a staff member, an interested citizen, a curious observer, or anyone else. Our aim is to explain the processes, terms, and functions most often employed in the two chambers of Congress to make our laws. Many works are available on the House and Senate; many focus on specific maneuvers or delve into the technical details, or go into the historic nature of the key attributes of each chamber. These are important works, but we want readers to be able to start with a clear and basic description of how business moves through each chamber. Each section of this book touches on topics about which much has been written and debated. We encourage you to seek out those works as well. Our goal is to provide an easygoing, conversational tour through the daily functions of this great legislative body and to provide enough information for you, the reader, to understand the vast majority of happenings on the House or Senate floors and form your own opinions about what you observe.

TWO

The House of Representatives
Where the Majority Party Rules

The United States House of Representatives is among the most transparent and representative legislative bodies in the world. All citizens have the right to call or visit their representative's offices and offer their opinions. Television cameras record and TV stations (and now the Internet) disseminate a variety of speeches, votes, debates, committee meetings, and other legislative actions of lawmakers. Records of representatives' opinions, statements, votes, and finances are publicly available and searchable. The floor of the House of Representatives is a manifestation of majority-ruled politics. Yet even with these transparent building blocks, the House of Representatives, like many other systems, has procedures so complex and evolving that few individuals are able to fully grasp the entirety of what goes on and to imagine how to impact the process.

The House is a majoritarian body, meaning a 50%+1 vote wins. Virtually everything that goes on in the House reflects the rule and agenda of the majority party. This is quite different from the Senate, which is less rigidly majoritarian. In the House, all administrative operations, political debates, and legislative processes are tightly controlled by the party in the majority, and expediency at the expense of the minority is not only a reality but an expanding governing doctrine of the chamber. Governance processes and principles are well documented and clearly defined by the majority party. At the beginning of each new Congress, the party in charge explicitly states the guiding principles and can make adjustments to the parliamentary procedures by which the House will be ruled for the next two-year/two-session Congress. The principles are made known in a long document called The Rules of the House of Representatives, itself a resolution commonly called "the rules package" that is passed on the opening day of the Congress.

The House rules for any particular Congress comprises procedural precedents dating back to Thomas Jefferson and the changes or new rules added to the document for each successive Congress. In addition to sometimes laying out a mechanism or processes for enacting the incoming majority party's upcoming legislative priorities, the rules package is filled with arcane procedural tools, totaling nearly 700 pages. Relatively few individuals have read and understand the entirety of that text, and so members are helped and advised by the House parliamentarians as well as the floor staffs representing the majority and minority parties, as they strategize and plan throughout the year.

THE WAYS AND MEANS AND APPROPRIATIONS COMMITTEES

> No Money shall be drawn from the Treasury, but in Consequence of Appropriations made by Law; and a regular Statement and Account of the Receipts and Expenditures of all public Money shall be published from time to time.
>
> *U.S. Constitution, Article 1, Section 9*

The legislative framework of the work done by the House is conducted in its committees. The House has established roughly twenty standing committees, a number of select committees, and a few joint committees with the Senate. The two most notable committees in the House are those that give it power over the national purse: the Ways and Means Committee and the Appropriations Committee. Historically, these have been the most powerful committees in the House as they define its most distinct constitutional duty. The Constitution explicitly grants to the House the exclusive privilege to levy taxes, and virtually all spending bills also must start in that chamber.

The historical genesis of this understanding dates back to the duties of its oldest committee—the Ways and Means Committee. As one of the House's first standing committees, it both levied taxes and disbursed the money for specific government functions. As the role of the federal government expanded so did the spending authority and burden on members to make extremely difficult and complicated choices. In 1865 Congress separated these two responsibilities, keeping taxation in the Ways and Means Committee and entrusting spending to a new body, the Appropriations Committee.

Both of these committees together shoulder the fundamental but monumentally difficult task of dealing with the country's finances and keeping the government solvent and working on a daily basis. The Ways and Means Committee is tasked with taxation and revenue. Taxes have long been created or abolished to change the flow of money among citizens, organizations, corporations, and the government.

The Appropriations Committee is the other great financial powerhouse of the House of Representatives. It has the jurisdiction to spend the government's revenues, to allocate financial discretionary resources to the executive branch to be disbursed on behalf of the American people for the administration, welfare, and common defense of the country. The Appropriations Committee is responsible for allocating the annual federal discretionary budget, agency by agency and program by program, in all the branches of government. This gives it unique oversight over the branches of government. Historically, Appropriations has been recognized as one of the most important committees in Congress because it is responsible for approving the amount of money that each federal program is allowed to spend on an annual basis. Since the committee is tasked with this oversight, it maintains a unique relationship with the other branches of government: it must fully understand how money is being spent so that it can make needed adjustments on an annual basis as the committee members see fit.

A significant development in recent years is that the importance of the Appropriations Committee has declined. First and foremost, the discretionary spending the committee oversees represents an ever-decreasing share of the annual federal budget as mandatory (or entitlement) spending has overtaken a greater share of the annual federal budget. Second, the House has recently abandoned the practice of ear-marking funds for particular programs, which in turn has led to less congressional control over the Executive Branch and a diminution of individual members' vested interest in the process. Mandatory spending—spending directed mostly toward entitlement programs such as Medicare, Medicaid, and Social Security—is allocated on an automatic basis by statute and not by the Appropriations Committee. Generally, authorizing committees, such as the House Committee on Energy and Commerce (and yes, the Ways and Means Committee), which oversee government programs, have jurisdiction over these programs; yet this automatic spending can only be changed by changing the original law that governs the level of spending.

What remains constant, however, is that the federal government must be funded (notwithstanding the occasional and momentary shutdown of operations in the · fall of 2013 and the late 1990s). So while earmarks may not currently be in practice, the Appropriations Committee will still be at work fulfilling its duty throughout the fiscal year.

THE CONGRESSIONAL CALENDAR

As is often the case, the theoretical process of how an idea becomes law is drastically more complicated when one attempts to put the theory into practice. There is a multistep protocol to present a bill and get it passed, but there is also a driving force that controls the available time to discuss legislation. On January 3 at twelve noon of each odd-numbered year when a new Congress begins, a rhythm is set in motion to purposefully build and add milestones to the majority party's carefully planned agenda for the two years ahead. The House leadership, using its rules and procedures to strategically execute items small and large, sets expectations early on to get members accustomed to a pattern. This institutionalized pattern can be understood through the congressional calendar publicized by the House Majority Leader.

We will dive deeper into the roles of leadership shortly, but the calendar, itself, has many layers of orchestrated timing. There is a plan for each day, week, month, quarter, year, term, and individual legislative priority. Driven by the Constitution, leadership priorities, unexpected crises, air travel, and holidays, the modern congressional calendar is both fluctuating and predictable. Specific operations and items may change in response to a variety of political or substantive challenges, but the general flow of the weekly calendar is influenced by committee schedules, constituents' desires to interact with their members, and the advent of commercial air travel. Today, the typical Washington work week for representatives is four to five days. When they are not in the District of Columbia, members are in their home districts meeting with constituents and being active in their communities. Many members of Congress spend countless hours on airplanes commuting between Washington and their districts. For those from rural districts west of the Mississippi River or states such as Hawaii or Alaska, this can mean multiple eight-to twelve-hour trips to spend a week in Washington followed by a single weekend in their home states. Travel schedules are carefully considered and accommodated when the Majority Leader crafts the weekly calendar (see a weekly schedule sample in appendix A).

The beginning of a Washington legislative week usually is not gaveled into session until after noon on the first day and provides an opportunity for the proverbial bed-check vote, which is held at 6:30 p.m. on a noncontroversial item in order to ensure that members find their way back to town by a certain time and date but don't require large policy briefings in advance. Typical bed-check votes are those that offer opportunities to send messages to constituents via miscellaneous and noncontroversial issues such as naming a post office, simple land exchanges, and small changes in law. These are largely bipartisan legislative efforts that have been agreed to between the majority and minority parties well in advance and often are signed into law. The end of every day that the House is in session—including this first day—is usually allocated for miscellaneous member speeches to be delivered on the floor.

Days 2, 3, 4, and sometimes 5, of the work week are when the real legislative action occurs. The second day of a legislative week is ordinarily used for more noncontroversial bills that resemble the first day's business, as well as the start of work on more serious measures. The final two or three days of the typical work week are reserved for dealing with the most difficult—national, and often partisan—issues. Although much work has been done for months or years in advance to hammer out details of major legislation, time on the floor still must be used to present and debate amendments, navigate procedural challenges from the minority, and execute votes. Often this process requires a full day or more before the vote on final passage.

If one zooms out to take in a full legislative year one can witness a series of events strategically positioned throughout the calendar. The president's budget request effectively kicks off the legislative year within the first two months. Due theoretically on the first Monday in February, the budget proposal can sometimes slip a few extra weeks or even months, especially for a new administration.

Authorizing committees, all committees but for the Appropriations Committee, will attempt to pass legislation ahead of the appropriations season so that their policy priorities are reflected in each individual appropriations bill. Thus, a substantial amount of authorizing activity—even if it does not result in new bills—will often take place in the late winter and spring months of a given year.

The appropriations process kicks into gear later in the spring and lasts until the end of the fiscal year—September 30, at least in theory. By that point, all appropriations work is supposed to be completed so that funding can be allocated for the coming fiscal year, beginning on October 1. However, meeting this deadline is rare in the modern Congresses, and the fall and early winter are needed to tie up loose ends that have been left over from both the authorizers and the appropriators.

It is important for you as an observer of Congress to recognize the basic breakdown of monthly activity so that you can anticipate not only what is happening in Congress but also the current agenda in the minds of staff and members.

THE LEGISLATIVE PROCESS

Members of the House of Representatives are the law-makers most directly representative of the population of the United States. In the 1st Congress there were sixty-five members, each one representing approximately 60,500 citizens based on 1790 census data. Over the years this ratio of citizens to representative held constant as the country grew, and the number of representatives also increased to accommodate the population. That changed with the Permanent Apportionment Act of 1929, when the maximum number of representatives was capped at the current limit of 435 members. Given U.S. population of approximately 324 million, if each member of the 114th Congress (2015–16) represented 60,500 people, the House of Representatives would be roughly 5,350 members. Instead, because of the Permanent Apportionment Act of 1929, there are on average 750,000 citizens for each member.

House members must understand the opinions, needs, problems, and priorities of their constituents. From this point of view, communication is an integral aspect of the legislative process. Internet, phones, and an advanced mail system have greatly increased long-distance connectivity, yet it proves a formidable challenge for a member to continuously communicate with (on average) three-quarters of a million people. To complicate the pure volume of constituents, as a practical matter, a plethora of widely varying priorities and issues face individuals every day. This puts a demand on elected officials to use a variety of tools and tactics to reach as many constituents—with a particular eye or focus towards active voters—in their respective districts as possible. This

toolbox includes legislative, communications, and advocacy tools such as special order and one-minute speeches
on the House floor (allowed at the beginning and end
of each legislative day), correspondence through letters
and e-mails, amendments in committee and on the
floor, committee report language, letters to the executive branch, actual votes, and, of course, the most well
known: the introduction of legislation. The lingo of
Capitol Hill is expansive and continues to evolve even
after more than 200 years of precedent and innovation.
This seemingly endless growth creates increasing opportunities for members to create and employ tactics
designed to drive their message home and, hopefully,
legislate successfully.

In a certain sense, introducing a bill or resolution is
part of the communication process and not just a step
toward making new law. Any representative can introduce legislation with relative ease through the help of
the House's Office of Legislative Counsel, which trans-
lates policy ideas into legal text. Bills are introduced for
a variety of reasons: to achieve some political result or to
introduce a new program or amend one, running the
gamut from small achievements to large-scale effects. Although most representatives understand that a bill they
introduce may not have a fighting chance of success in
the year it is introduced (or even the next), introducing
it serves as a statement of purpose for that member of
Congress and his or her constituents. The issue in question likely has a direct impact to the district and the
member recognizes that his or her constituents would
like to consider legislative fixes to the problem and want
to know that the representative is on the case. As soon
as the bill is filed, it is officially recorded in the *Congres-*

sional Record. It can be examined by outside groups and other members, and it provides a permanent record that the issue is a priority for that representative. Over time as that issue or member becomes more prominent, the possibility of real action may increase. More often than not, a substantive legislative initiative takes many years of revision, research, often multiple champions, a coalition of support, and sometimes a political crisis before it can become law.

When a bill is introduced, the Speaker of the House refers it to the committee or committees of jurisdiction under which the language of the legislation falls. For example, a bill about occupational safety would be sent to the Education and the Workforce Committee to review. For all bills, the House rules on committee referrals are designed to comport with committee jurisdictions and facilitate an efficient consideration of the chamber's legislative business. The Office of the Parliamentarian provides the House with nonpartisan guidance on parliamentary rules and procedures. The House parliamentarian, assisted by a staff of lawyers, is charged with processing, keeping track of and moving forward the large volume of legislation. The Speaker's and House parliamentarian's staffs work closely together, from referring bills to the proper committee to deciding how the House floor is officiated when a bill is being considered. (This process creates a veritable hurricane of paperwork for the governing party. Generally 10,000 to 15,000 bills are introduced in each Congress, but only a handful get serious consideration by any committee responsible for moving the legislation to a full House vote.)

Once a bill has been referred to the appropriate committee, that body leads the effort to review, revise, and report back the legislation to the full House chamber for its consideration—called reporting the bill out of committee. Often, legislation is expansive and covers many issues. In cases where the legislation has relevance to multiple jurisdictions, the Speaker of the House refers the matter to multiple committees. He or she can do this in a variety of ways:

* A sequential referral. This is the simplest and most common approach. After the committee with primary jurisdiction has concluded its review and reported the matter out, the legislation is referred to additional committees in a specific sequence.

* A concurrent referral. A primary committee is designated, but the legislation is concurrently referred to another committee, and both may report out once business on the bill has been concluded.

* A simultaneous referral to multiple committees. This is very rare.

In addition, the Speaker may impose time limitations on referrals, refer matters to special or ad hoc committees, and refer just portions of the legislation rather than the whole matter. The reality is that most bills are never seriously considered by any committee. Of bills that get considered, just a fraction are actually reported out of committee and passed by the House. If they pass in the House, they are sent to the Senate to run the gauntlet of committee work and floor activity there. On average only 3 to 5 percent of the bills filed in each Congress become law.

As an administrative matter, the massive volume of bills and requests for time on the floor require the Speaker to employ a variety of procedural rules to maintain a constant but controlled legislative environment for all members. In addition to the day-to-day operations, the Speaker must be consistent in reminding his or her constituency of the party's priorities and the party's vision as to what would serve the nation best. The rules package written and approved by each individual Congress not only serves as a road map for the House leadership to plan to deal with administrative issues and daily requests, but also can set out the national priorities for the coming two-year term.

LEADERSHIP STRUCTURE

In each chamber of Congress a select few are part of a leadership team of each party. The most important positions in the House stay constant: Speaker of the House, majority leader (and minority leader), majority whip (and minority whip), and conference chair (or caucus chair).

Leadership positions in the House of Representatives have evolved and possess unique powers. Each individual in the majority party's leadership is entitled to play an integral role in governing the chamber and moving priorities forward. The minority's positions act as shadow leadership, representing their conference or caucus members, often in opposition to the majority party's agenda. Both parties independently recognize certain members by electing them to party leadership positions.

This accolade is not an endorsement of their independent thinking but instead a charge to carry forth the collective mission in the name of the party. In fact, all but one of these positions is elected by party members in advance of the opening day of each Congress (the beginning of the calendar year). The only position elected by a simple majority of the whole House is the Speaker of the House (after he or she is nominated within the conference or caucus).

We here present an outline of the key leadership positions of the House as seen through the lens of the majority party. The minority party has nearly all of the same positions, with the exception of the Speaker, but they have less power and a different charge as alluded to above.

The Speaker is the most powerful position in the House of Representatives, and is the only officer of the House specifically mentioned by the U.S. Constitution, although the language does mention electing other officers. Article 1, Section 2, instructs that the House shall choose their Speaker, and each of the members casts a vote on the opening day of the new Congress to elect a new Speaker. The individual achieving a majority of those present and voting is elected Speaker. If no one meets that threshold with the first vote, the House votes again until a Speaker is elected. This process is inherently partisan and can be contentious even within each party. In the distant past, it has caused major delays in the official opening of a new Congress.

All other leadership positions are functions of party organization. The Speaker is second in the presidential line of succession, after the vice president. As the head of the majority party, the Speaker is the main conduit for the majority to the Senate and the White House.

The Speaker has both operational and legislative authority. Some of the Speaker's operational roles are not well known. The Speaker selects candidates for administrative offices of the House: the clerk, parliamentarian, chaplain, sergeant-at-arms, and chief accountability officer, among others. Technically, these positions are elected by all the members of the House, but the Speaker's preference carries a great deal of weight, and generally the Speaker's chosen candidates are approved by the House.

On the legislative side, the Speaker's greatest power is that of presiding over the House. The Speaker opens the House for legislative business each day, selects the chairman of the Rules Committee at the beginning of each Congress, and generally oversees the legislative operations of the House as conducted by the clerk and refereed by the House parliamentarian.

The Speaker is also charged with leading his or her party organization and establishing the broad governing agenda. Think of the Speaker as the head coach of a sports team whose players are the members of the majority party.

The Speaker also has internal party powers. One of the most influential of the Speaker's internal party powers is as chair of the Steering Committee, the committee responsible for selecting all committee chairmen (who will be members of the majority party) and also making committee assignments for each member of his or her party. In theory, committee chairmen are voted on by all members of the Steering Committee; in practice, however, the Speaker has more votes than any other member of the Steering Committee and so can

significantly sway the ultimate outcome of these place-
ments. This enables party leadership—as overseen by
the Speaker—to tightly control the actions of committee chairs in favor of acting in the best interest of the
party's legislative agenda. The Speaker is also charged
with settling internal party disputes, approving all
member travel, and providing for various other daily
housekeeping matters.

The other three main leadership positions—majority
leader, whip, and conference (or caucus) chair—act as
assistant coaches to the Speaker. The majority leader's
primary function is to set the House's legislative agenda
and schedule. This means overseeing committees to ensure they are producing legislation in a timely fashion
that conforms with the majority's legislative vision. The
majority leader then controls the movement of legislation on the House floor, designating when and what
bills are considered and voted on during any given day.
Of most importance to members' quality of life in office,
the leader determines the House's daily schedule—when
votes are taken and ultimately, when the work for the
week has concluded.

The whip is the party's chief vote counter. Whereas
the Speaker lays out an overall vision and the majority
leader helps craft that vision into concrete legislation,
the whip is responsible for ensuring that each bill can
pass. The whip advises the Speaker and majority leader
on changes to legislation needed to ensure passage of
that legislation. In order to push passage of a bill, the
whip often participates in some horse trading with individual members to round up support. Since the whip
spends an inordinate amount of time on vote counting,
he or she is often the person most attuned to the views

of individual members and most able to communicate those views back to the Speaker and the majority leader.

Within the House each party has a sub-organization, the Democratic caucus and the Republican conference, where party members can meet in private, so to speak. The conference or caucus chair is charged with crafting the public message for the party. Thus, the chair communicates why specific legislation is good for the country as a whole and also for members' constituents.

Below the conference or caucus chair are numerous leadership positions on each side of the aisle. However, the four positions just described represent the core functions and resources of party leadership in the House.

THE RULES COMMITTEE

The Rules Committee is fundamentally a tool of leadership. Its chair is appointed by the Speaker and has a seat at the leadership table and on the Steering Committee. This makes the chair of the Rules Committee not just beholden to leadership, but also part of leadership.

The Rules Committee functions as the governing body of the majority in the House of Representatives in order to set and control the process by which legislation is considered on the floor. The committee oversees the legislative administration of the House and also deploys the majority party's tactics to guide policy priorities onto the floor so as to ensure the most likely path toward a smooth debate, successful amendment process, and ultimately, passage. In other words, the committee spends most of its time acting as the majority leadership's traffic manager so that the party's most important legislation comes to the House floor in an efficient manner and is enacted. The committee structures debate through the process of selecting amendments to bills. This selection process is intended to allow a variety of ideas to be heard while still promoting the majority's argument, and it also makes sure that legislation passes the floor in a form intended by the majority leadership. The Rules Committee also has some limited legislative jurisdiction; for example, it has authority to structure unique legislative processes like trade promotion authority (TPA).

To guarantee that these objectives are met, the Rules Committee is stacked heavily in the majority's favor and populated by members who are most likely to support the leadership's agenda. Behind the scenes, the staff of the Rules Committee and of the leadership work to process amendments, sometimes sifting through hundreds of proposals per bill, weeding out those that would have the most dire impact for the proposed legislation while seeking to promote as wide of a debate as possible.

RULES OF THE HOUSE

For months in advance of each new Congress the members of the majority work on a new rules package— updates and changes to the existing Rules of the House. It is an imprint of the governing majority party's priorities and is used as a legislative enabler for the coming two years of legislative activity. Very forward thinking and reflective of a legislative strategy and procedural process, each Congress's rules are passed during the opening week (on or around January 3) and include a framework to address priorities, matters of political significance, and unforeseen national crises.

In addition to reflecting partisan politics of the day, this massive document also reflects years of parliamentary precedent dating back more than two hundred years. At its core, it is a base of procedural practice by which the House conducts its legislative business. Consequently, it is not surprising that all rules packages contain many of the same rules from Congresses prior. In fact, the incoming majority party usually passes the previous Congress's rules, with fine-tuned amendments that serve the purposes outlined earlier. Using many of the tools contained in the House Rules document, the Rules Committee writes special rules tailored to each bill under consideration. These rules are colored by the principle of germaneness, which requires that there must be a genuine connection between any proposed amendment and the original text and intent of the bill (for example, adding language about gun rights to an education bill would violate the principle of germaneness). This requirement does not necessarily relate directly to the jurisdiction of the committees. Its purpose is more narrow: to maintain the original focus and purpose of legislation. Although this rule is governed by the House parliamentarian, the Rules Committee still decides which amendments may be considered. As a practical and political messaging opportunity, sometimes members will knowingly offer an amendment that is nongermane only to have a point of order raised against its consideration. During the unwieldy appropriations season (which we will shortly explain), offering a nongermane amendment on the floor can be an effective surprise tactic by the minority and individual members seeking to make political points. These legislative surprises are mostly avoided, however, as the process for which the vast majority of substantive legislation is considered on the floor is controlled by the Rules Committee. The Committee may grant exceptions to these written rules, a process known as providing a waiver, though again, the majority tightly choreographs such instances.

What observers will find is that the Rules Committee is fundamental to the passage of the majority party's legislative priorities in the House. It is an integral source of order and due diligence given the enormous number of requests that can arise from 435 representatives. At its core, the House is an efficient legislative body and the Rules Committee helps enable and strengthen that key and defining characteristic.

TYPES OF SPECIAL RULES

Four types of special rules are applied by the Rules Committee to bills brought to the House floor: open, modified open, structured, and closed. These rules represent a spectrum of amend-ability ranging from any amendments may be offered to none whatsoever. When the Rules Committee meets, it must prescribe the type of rule for the piece of legislation before it that will most effectively benefit the ruling party's priorities and reach the preferred outcome. Based on the committee process to date, the majority often knows what types of amendments to expect from the membership and is broadly aware of how the minority might respond on a given

bill. The process on the floor of the House of Representatives is almost entirely choreographed in advance,
largely controlled by the Speaker and majority leader
and governed by the rule issued by the Rules Committee specific to that bill.

Open Rule

The most flexible type of rule is the open rule. When a
bill is governed by an open rule, germane amendments
may be offered by any representative during consideration of the bill on the floor of the House. In other
words, the open rule means that there is no prescriptive
process by the majority (aside from the House rules) and
that all House members have the right to alter the language of the bill so long as their amendments are germane. The original bill text could be repeatedly and indefinitely altered by members suggesting a change, and
the bill, reflecting that change, is ultimately voted on by
the whole House. As a matter of party politics, this is an
extremely dangerous proposition and would allow the
minority to offer amendments difficult to deny by the
majority, sometimes significantly changing the intention
of the original bill. Tightly written and narrowly focused
legislation can be considered under open rules because
the principle of germaneness removes much of the opportunity to alter the substance of the bill. Interestingly,
this open process is what almost every minority party
promises to revive when appealing to voters during campaigns—a more open process and more open rules.

One category of bills that is historically brought to
the floor under an open rule is the twelve general appropriations bills. Appropriations bills are generally

considered under an open rule because of a prescriptive process given to privileged business, issues considered to be so important that they are effectively exempt from the regular order of business and can be reported directly to the calendar. The basic procedure with appropriations is explained in more detail in the section called Committee of the Whole—a committee whose membership is all of the members of the House. What makes an open rule manageable on an appropriations bill from a majority leadership perspective is a pre-existing House rule that prohibits legislating on an appropriations bill. So while any member can offer an amendment on the floor under an open rule on an appropriations bill, they only have the ability to change (or prohibit) funding levels.

Modified Open Rule

The modified open rule is designed to still allow a lot of engagement by the minority party, but eliminate the element of surprise by requiring that only amendments pre-printed in the *Congressional Record* can be considered. A member introducing an amendment must usually submit the text of the proposal one day in advance in order to have it printed in the *Congressional Record*. Though it may seem an unnecessary inconvenience, the advance notice of legislative proposals gives additional preparation time for the leadership to plan the legislative day and devise a strategy for promoting or opposing each amendment.

It is in the interest of majority leadership to give its own membership public legislative success while protecting the intent of legislation. Modifying an open rule with a pre-printing requirement helps promote this goal. For example, suppose an amendment offered by the minority proves popular enough to pass with some support from the majority party. The leadership could arrange ahead of time for one of its own party members to submit a similar amendment that is less detrimental to the intent of the underlying legislation, which, if successfully passed, would then enable the leadership to defeat the minority's more destructive amendment.

Further, the requirement to record amendments in the *Congressional Record* also provides time for congressional monitors such as the Budget Committee and the Congressional Budget Office to do due diligence on budgetary implications of each amendment on the bill. In short, a modified open rule allows for a more open process but with a more controlled and efficient environment on the floor. Modified open rules can also be used to set caps on the amount of time allowed for debate on each amendment.

Structured and Closed Rules

Structured and closed rules are quite similar, but although the two terms are sometimes used interchangeably, they definitely serve distinct purposes.

A structured rule is vetted entirely by the Rules Committee, and all amendments allowed for consideration must be approved by the committee and listed within the text of the rule itself. The approved amendments are also given a specific allocation of debate time for consideration (for a sample of a structured rule, see appendix B).

In a closed rule no amendments can be offered. All changes to the bill must have been made in the committee process or added by the Rules Committee. There can be no changes to the bill once it reaches the floor, and a simple up-or-down vote is allowed with the opportunity for the minority to offer a substitute.

Structured and closed rules share many principles, and are most popularly used by the majority leadership when they wish to tightly protect the intent of a piece of legislation and move it forward in as efficient a manner as possible. Such legislation is generally considered partisan by the minority party. There are some exceptions to this generalization. A good example would be foreign policy issues when national security is at stake. Leadership will often use a structured or closed rule in these cases, not because the legislation is partisan, but actually to protect it from becoming partisan. One of these rules protects members from taking a difficult political vote that is seemingly popular in a campaign ad, for example, but could have devastating consequences. This creates an interesting dichotomy where these rules are used for both extremely partisan legislation and difficult substantive legislation.

COMMITTEE OF THE WHOLE

The Committee of the Whole—of the whole House, that is—is a tool commonly used by the majority party to gain legislative efficiency. The procedural rules for Committee of the Whole meetings are different from those of other business conducted on the floor of the House; such meetings proceed as a collegiate discussion with questions and answers, rather than as a sequence of speeches each with minimal interruption from other members and strictly moderated by the speaker.

Normally each House committee sets its own rules as decided by a majority of the membership. Likewise, the majority ruling party decides the rules for the Committee of the Whole. The Committee of the Whole meets in the House chamber but has no quorum requirements and can limit the time of debate for amendments in order to speed through them as quickly as possible. There are two quick ways for onlookers to tell when they are seeing the House function as the House and when it functions as this committee: The person sitting in the Speaker's chair is recognized as the committee chair and the mace is on the floor; when the House is in session the person sitting in the Speaker's chair is recognized as the Speaker and the mace is closer to the rostrum.

This process also plays an important role in consolidating the amount of time each member must go to the floor for votes by allowing for the rolling of votes into a series during a session of the entire House. These series allow for quick sets of votes on related items. Usually all of the requested recorded votes from previous items, the motion to recommit (a final amendment), and then final passage on the bill will be handled as the full House. Observers will most commonly see the House sitting in the Committee of the Whole for the consideration of appropriations bills.

FLOOR PROCEDURE

As we've discussed, the process of bringing legislation to the House floor for consideration and a vote is controlled by the majority party, and a number of different procedures are employed to control what happens to legislation both before and after it reaches the House floor.

The majority leader acts as the gatekeeper of legislation in the House and schedules what happens on the floor. He or she decides when the House will be in session, what the hourly schedule will be, and, most important, what legislation the House will consider. The majority leader, in consultation with the Speaker and the majority whip, sets the legislative agenda and decides on the procedures to invoke.

The majority leadership can choose from five legislative procedures when deciding which bills will come to the House floor: unanimous consent, suspension of the rules, special rules (described previously), privileged business, and discharge petition. Unanimous consent and suspension of the rules are used for noncontroversial legislation. Unanimous consent is when the majority and minority parties jointly agree to bring up a piece of legislation and, further, agree on the parameters for its consideration—for example, debate time and amendments. In order for a unanimous consent agreement to be formalized, the House must approve of the agreement. If any one member objects, the agreement as to the procedure does not proceed, and the legislation, too, does not proceed.

Suspension of the rules is used similarly, although the full support of the House is not the standard for consideration of a bill under suspension of the rules. House Rules allow for suspensions, that is, legislation considered using this mechanism, on specific legislative days, usually Mondays, Tuesdays, and Wednesdays. House Rules prescribe that suspensions will be considered with forty minutes of debate time, equally divided between the majority and minority, with no amendments allowed. An up-or-down vote on passage is taken at the end of the forty minutes, with one important caveat: in order for the legislation to pass, two-thirds of those present and voting must approve, rather than a simple majority. In a full House of 435 members, this means 290 must vote yes for the legislation to pass. Thus, while the vote does not need to be unanimous, it must enjoy healthy bipartisan support.

Most often, special rules are used by the majority leadership when substantive legislation is under consideration. As discussed in earlier sections on the Rules Committee and the types of rules, this tactic allows the majority party, through the Speaker-controlled Rules Committee, to set the party's terms for consideration. This mechanism does not preclude the legislation from having bipartisan support, but it does protect the legislation from minority or individual member input that the majority does not prefer.

The final two mechanisms for bringing legislation to the floor are tactics that the minority or rank-and-file members can employ without the consent of the majority leader or majority leadership. The first is legislation or other business brought under the rubric of privileged business. There are a number of issues that House Rules deem privileged in the House and that can therefore be raised should the offering member meet certain standards. One notable matter reaching the privileged threshold that is often employed by the minority party is anything affecting the dignity of the House. These are commonly referred to as privileged resolutions and are often offered by the minority leader as he or she can gain recognition on the same day (rather than rank-and-file members who must wait a number of days of the majority leader's choosing). Such resolutions are about the conduct of the House and are usually designed to highlight ethical issues or matters that the minority party believes the majority is overlooking, to the detriment of the House and, ultimately, the country.

Last, a discharge petition can be used by rank-and-file members from both parties (though more likely by members from the minority) to force specific legislation out of committee and onto the floor. House Rules allow for discharge petitions to be filed on any bill or resolution; the Clerk of the House keeps a tally of those that are filed. In order for the bill or resolution to come to the floor, 218 members of the House must sign the discharge petition. This can be a long process, and so it is not rare for many discharge petitions to be pending with the Clerk throughout any given Congress. Since the threshold for the legislation coming to the floor is a majority of members signing the petition, the minority's petitions generally are not successful. But they use the mechanism anyhow because starting a particular petition may help to highlight an issue the minority believes the majority is ignoring. Should a discharge petition come close to being successful, the majority leadership itself will usually author a similar petition, but under their chosen parameters so as to supersede the discharge petition.

THREE

The Senate

Where Debate and Deals Rule

The Senate is a significantly different body from the House. The founders designed the system to have House members serve two years, a president serve four years, and senators serve six years. Having two-thirds of the membership of the Senate remain unchanged after an election allows for some stability and institutional knowledge across the government. This creates specific life cycles of time and pressure for each chamber, impacting how each works. There is considerable literature and discussion on the continuous nature of the Senate, the ways that affect potential rules changes, and the living nature of the Senate in general. For Senate lovers, we urge you to seek out these writings as they are an important part of the discussions about the evolving Senate.

The election pattern for Senate seats, whereby just one-third of the seats are open in any election year, ensures that even if the presidency and the House change parties in an election, at least two-thirds of the previous senators will still be serving, even if under different leadership. In contrast to the House, where the party in the majority holds clear sway over almost everything, the Senate is a forum for extended debate, and political minorities can find ways to exercise considerable power. In addition to the structural differences between the chambers (election cycles, term length, two senators per state regardless of size), the Senate—while having the same oversight and legislative tasks as the House—is also tasked with "Executive Calendar" items that the House is not. The Senate, for instance, has an advise-and-consent role over nominations and treaties sent by the president. This is an additional factor when thinking through floor time and planning for the Senate calendar.

The majority sets the agenda for the Senate but the minority power is a hallmark of the institution. Minority in the Senate context can mean a few different things. The usual meaning of "the minority" is the political party that controls fewer seats in the chamber. The minority on any given issue may mean not the minority party but, rather, a group of senators from both sides of the aisle who, for parochial or philosophical reasons, disagree with what a majority is attempting to move forward and seek to debate the issue further, or indefinitely. The Senate is often seen as a place of long-standing traditions with a rich debate history, insulated from some of the passions and political winds or daily changes and news cycle that can drive some of the House's energy. But the extent to which it is impacted by the crisis or debates of the day is growing and also the subject of much discussion of the modern Senate.

Since the Senate is a long-run operation, where members will have six years, and often more, to work, seniority and constant negotiations are especially important in the management and running of the chamber. For example, members' seniority, work, and geography are all taken into consideration in fulfilling their respective requests. The time that a senator has served can impact many things: earlier choice of office space, better desk selection, and, potentially, committee assignments, chair or ranking memberships, leadership, or other caucus assignments. With only 100 members, the personal promises, personalities, negotiations, and actions of each member make a big difference—especially as senators navigate deals within the parties and across the full chamber.

At its core, the Senate is a place of constant dance between majority and minority. Each member has power and thus the leadership teams of both parties create strategy with their members' views in mind, and must balance many conflicting demands with the demands of a functioning Senate. The Senate is also defined by being a place of relatively few rules compared to the House—designed for open debate and open amendments, and for deal making among members. The members guide the body, as each leadership team must gauge what the needs and wants of their membership are, and then frame their cross-party negotiations, as by their nature negotiations are a pain-and-gain trade-off. For party leaderships, that calculation is based on their members and the goal of any given discourse. For example, if a nomination is highly controversial, one party may decide to use all of its available tools to protest. Or, for example, if a bill is a must-pass emergency item, each party will factor that into its thinking about how to approach the floor. *Context always matters.* The majority and minority each have different tools to express their vision of governance and what they seek to convey to their constituents.

Each caucus (party) must discuss and find what the needs are within their own membership, and then negotiate between parties. In this way, all 100 members, and all 50 states, have sway over Senate happenings. This dynamic is a main driver of the Senate. It must also be viewed more broadly within the context of who controls the White House and House of Representatives, and who holds majority in the Senate. These dynamics also impact negotiations and Senate work flows. For example, the majority party in the Senate controls the chairmanships of committees, and decisions as to what will be marked up, in addition to having the first say in what comes to the floor. These majority-minority dynamics also help decode what is happening on the Senate floor at any given time.

BASICS OF LEGISLATION IN THE SENATE

The Senate floor is fluid, and members often have to stay flexible since negotiations are ongoing. What follows offers the basics in an academic sense, to enable the reader to track and understand the daily Senate flow. From here, we encourage you to seek out the many wonderful primary and secondary sources that provide the full range of Senate background, rules, and explanation. The Senate website itself is a wealth of information about the Senate standing rules, floor, desks, history, procedure, and proceedings, and there are seminal works such as Martin B. Gold's *Senate Procedure and Practice*, in addition to a myriad of writings and lectures from all ends of the spectrum on the Senate and its ways. For procedural sources, see rules.senate.gov or read *Riddick's Rules of Procedure*.

The Senate is meant to be open—open debate, open amendments. But the reality is more complex as much has to be considered. Two terms are in constant use in discussions of paths whereby bills move through the Senate: "cloture" and "unanimous consent." These two terms are the mechanisms that enable legislation before the Senate to move—swiftly if there is cooperation or slowly if not. Some combination of the two is often used.

Unanimous consent, often referred to simply as consent, is a term in the Senate used to describe the process by which items are passed or confirmed without objection from any senator—a shorthand for deals, large and small. It may also refer to a process by which a deal has actively been made on the floor to move an item forward with some structure for debate and specific timing. For example, a bill can be finished with a consent agreement or by the filing of cloture. (See samples in appendix C of a "hotline" asking for every member to agree to a proposed resolution.)

Cloture is a mechanism by which debate is ended on a bill with a three-fifths vote of the Senate, and any further debate must be limited to just thirty hours. It is the key procedure by which the Senate can vote to place a time limit on consideration of a bill or other matter. As such it is a brake on both filibusters (a tactic explained later but generally used to obstruct progress on an item) and also the unfettered debate that is a hallmark of the way business is done in the Senate.

In the Senate most bills are passed through the unanimous consent system rather than needing lengthy floor debate time, and this greatly impacts how bills are drafted and negotiated. Senators are aware that the best chance for a bill is to clear by consent, or to have enough consensus to be able to be included in a package of bills. To petition the majority leader for valuable floor time is a gamble, as he or she will always have several competing pressures. The bills and nominations that do get processed through formal floor consideration typically follow a few routes discussed in later sections. It can take a week for a bill to die in the Senate, let alone for a bill to survive and pass. The majority leader must juggle these time factors if the Senate is to get all of its planned work done.

THE SENATE CALENDAR AND CONSIDERATIONS OF TIME

In the Senate, bills can often take a week or more to be debated on the floor, and procedural maneuvers can potentially burn up floor debate time without producing substantive legislative advancements. In addition to the basic bill, there are several types of items which need time for consideration such as Senate and House bills, House messages, and resolutions: joint resolutions, concurrent resolutions, and run-of-the-mill resolutions. In congressional jargon all of the aforementioned actions are called "vehicles" which can be broadly defined as a legislative tool. In addition to the time requirements of the floor, senators themselves are pressed for time. Essentially, to envision the pressures on each senator, think of them as the center of a wheel with several spokes—the spokes being their state and constituents and their desire to serve them through the tools of the Senate, their floor obligations, their committee assignments, their caucus assignments, their fundraisers, their families, and their personal stories or interests (for example, a senator may be very interested in foreign policy after living abroad, or in climate due to his or her state's geography). Giving the appropriate amount of time or energy to each activity and interest can be an additional challenge for senators and their staffs.

In addition to all of that, the majority party members have the added obligation of presiding over the Senate. Technically the vice president is the presiding officer of the Senate (and the intersection between the executive and legislative branches), but the vice president is busy and cannot be on the floor all the time. He or she chiefly appears on the floor to break tied votes, sometimes preside over high-profile votes, and swear in new senators. The most senior member of the majority party then stands in as the president of the Senate and is called the president pro tempore, but because that senator likely chairs a committee and has many other obligations, the presiding chair is typically filled with younger members of the majority. In this way younger members get training on the workings of the Senate floor and parliamentary procedure. But most important, filling the presiding chair is one of the ways that the majority exerts its control over the Senate floor, as there is always a member of the majority party present on the floor.

Often, new Senate watchers or staff are frustrated as they attempt to follow what is happening in the Senate purely on the basis of reading the Senate rules. In reality, the Senate is meant to be a place of open debate, and it is run very much by the 100 senators. Consequently, what usually happens is a combination of rules and deals—the rules are used to create pressure points, and then deals are done, so consent agreements end up ruling the day and can make almost anything happen. If you read and apply the rules while accounting for context, you will usually be able to accurately track Senate happenings, though not always. In a fluid body, 20 percent of the material covers 80 percent of the time, but sometimes there will see a fancy and rare maneuver or sometimes the context will surprise.

In addition to the procedural importance of the maneuver, the history of cloture and the filibuster in the Senate is fascinating—in particular, the pressure points in great debates of the last century where the cloture thresholds saw creation and then change. Senate.gov documents the change in frequency of use of the filibuster and cloture filings over the years and has background on the maneuver. There are also extensive academic articles on the Senate and the filibuster. No conversation about the Senate is complete without a contemplation of the filibuster and its implications.

The Use of Cloture

The best way to illustrate the complexity and time necessary to complete cloture is to run through examples. If a bill is to be considered on Monday with a consent agreement and some senators do not like it, they tell the leaders that they cannot give a consent agreement for its speedy consideration at that time. The leaders will communicate this to each other directly or through their floor staffs. Knowing that, the majority leader will begin the process "by the book"—with cloture. This gives the leader the most options: a by-the-book timeline or the possibility of deals later in the process.

This process begins by filing cloture on the motion to proceed. Once the motion to proceed has been adopted—or in some cases where the motion to proceed is not debatable—cloture may be filed on the vehicle itself. The cloture timeline can be a source of some confusion. Three common samples are below, for substitute amendments, privileged vehicles, and nominations.

Cloture timeline with a substitute amendment   Often, there is a more complicated process for cloture when there is also a substitute amendment drafted with some changes to the policy that help garner more votes. This can mean that the substitute amendment is not germane to the original underlying bill text because the scope is usually expanded in deal making. This creates the following timeline:

Day 1: Cloture filed on both the substitute amendment and on the underlying bill that it will amend.

Day 2: The intervening day on both cloture petitions.

Day 3: Cloture ripens (meaning a vote is now allowed) on the first petition (on the substitute amendment), one hour after the Senate convenes. If cloture is invoked by garnering sixty votes (or three-fifths of the Senate) or more, there may be up to thirty hours of debate prior to an adoption vote on the substitute amendment with a simple majority threshold. Immediately after that adoption vote, the cloture vote on the underlying bill (now as amended by the substitute amendment) ripens for a vote (at a

60-vote threshold). If cloture is invoked, there is again up to thirty hours post-cloture debate prior to a passage vote. If cloture is not invoked on the first petition (on the substitute amendment), the second cloture petition (on the original bill) immediately ripens for a vote and the normal process continues. Note that in the case of failed cloture votes, motions to reconsider can be entered so the votes can happen again, in case there is future progress.

Cloture on a privileged vehicle (message vehicles or conference reports).

Day 1: Cloture filed on a conference report.

Day 2: The intervening day on that cloture petition.

Day 3: One hour after the Senate convenes, the cloture petition ripens for a vote. If cloture is invoked, there may be up to thirty hours post-cloture prior to an adoption by simple majority vote on the conference report.

Cloture on nominations.

Day 1: Cloture petitions filed on, for example, three nominations.

Day 2: Intervening day on all three cloture petitions.

Day 3: Cloture ripens on petition no. 1, one hour after the Senate convenes (requiring majority vote for all nominations). If cloture is invoked, it is subject to up to thirty hours of post-cloture debate prior to a confirmation vote (majority threshold).

Once the first cloture petition is complete or cloture is not invoked on it, the next cloture petition immediately ripens for a vote and the process repeats.

Note that the Senate can conduct other business on days 1 and 2 of the cloture process. Once the Senate invokes cloture and is in post-cloture debate on a matter, it cannot consider other items except by consent. Cloture is designed to focus the Senate on a matter and allow for the last hours of debate. Absent cloture, the Senate can potentially debate a matter endlessly. Also of note, when the Senate is post-cloture, the nature of debate changes. Whereas it is usually relatively free-flowing and senators can use as many hours as they need, in the post-cloture thirty hours, each member starts by only controlling an hour. If they seek more, it must be yielded to them by the majority or minority leaders, or floor managers, and even they can only control up to three hours each. If no senator seeks to be recognized to speak in the post-cloture time, the question at hand may be called. The time can also be yielded with cooperation.

What often happens during the cloture process is that sometime during those days, a deal comes together. Perhaps after day 3, when it is shown that the bill has more than sixty votes to move forward, those who did not like it decide that although they still plan to vote no and speak against it; they do not need to use more time on a bill that has shown it has the votes to succeed, so a consent agreement comes together to vote early instead of waiting until all post-cloture debate is over. Or, if no one seeks to speak during debate, any member with a

sufficient second (that is having at least eleven other senators voice their support) may attempt to call for the vote,
which may take place before the thirty hours are up. Or
perhaps the leaders find a way to make a deal with the
senators who do not like the bill, to fix their issues at a later
time or hold a hearing, or support a letter, or some other
promise, and so they allow a consent agreement and passage vote. Or perhaps there is no deal, and the bill process
finishes "by the book" with all debate time being used.

Things can go many ways and that was the plan for
the Senate: that each member can sway things or call
attention to the issues he or she cares about on any given
item, and that a group of senators are able to extend debate. Senators have time to make their case, and despite
the existence of rules to help structure debate and give
members distinct tools to maneuver, in the end the process is a mix of procedure and politics. To understand
what is happening on the floor, you have to see what is
happening in terms of this mix. They tango together.
The rules create the outlines and pressure points that
then often collapse into deals. The rules cannot be read
in a vacuum: always look to the context, what is happening on the floor, what are the politics, policies, and
personalities involved. It's a complex mixture of the
three. Or in cases where things are moving strictly by the
book, that is also a choice and usually signifies something
beyond the fact itself.

Life Cycles in the Senate

Time and timing are a big part of the legislative dance.
Time is what the majority needs and the minority can
use, and it affects what the majority leader can—or

cannot—bring to the floor. Thus, it is helpful to think of the impact of time on the flow of Senate business by chunks of time. The basic unit of time in the Congress is . . . a Congress. That is, Congress is also a time expression. Each Congress lasts two years, and is numbered. Each year of a Congress is called a session: session 1 and session 2. Thus, the unit of time called a Congress is defined by the shortest election cycle, the two-year cycle whereby all members of the House stand for election. A senator serves for three Congresses before she stands for election again, and in this way a Senate term has its own life cycle.

A year in the Senate   The flow of Senate business is broken down by holidays, recess dates, and regular annual deadlines such as October 1, the start of the new fiscal year, or the day the debt limit must be raised, or the day the highway bill must be reauthorized, to name a few. All such events help to create pressure points.

The month and session   The word "session" also has a second meaning: each chamber of Congress has additional cuts of time called "being in session," which are largely set by the majority leaderships. Some Senate sessions are just a few days or weeks, most are several weeks. Each such session has its own flow, a target as to how much can get done, what needs to get done, how much time things end up actually taking, and so forth.

The week   Generally, the Senate's work week goes from Monday through Thursday in Washington, but can go longer if enough has not been accomplished to please the majority leader. He or she may threaten to keep members in Washington through Friday or beyond to create pressure for consent agreements or votes, especially if there is a deadline looming that must be met. Friday session often means that something is urgent or requires a lot of debate before it can be processed, as senators are often eager to return to their constituents and work in their respective states.

The day   The day usually starts with an hour devoted to morning business, during which senators can discuss any issue, not just the bill being debated. The Senate then proceeds to debate the issues on the floor and takes any other votes needed. Before adjourning for the day, consent is used to set up the schedule for the next day. Absent consent agreements, the Senate day can have tense or unpredictable moments, or can appear slow as negotiations continue. The saying "still waters run deep" often seems to apply to the Senate day. It may seem like the day is simply filled with floor statements, often unrelated, but usually negotiations are taking place about how to move forward on a bill or nomination that will come to fruition hours or days later. The floor statements often also play a part in the theater unfolding behind the scenes to help move or hold up legislation.

Day-by-day work   Each year, month, and week has its own rough calendar; in the Senate individual weeks can have particular emphasis. This is directly related to the slow burn of the Senate; while in the House a number of big items may be happening all in one week, the Senate tends to work on one large item on the floor and spend one or two weeks on that item. There are, however, exceptions to that pattern, especially toward the end of a year or a Congress, when the Senate is under pressure to finish several items at once. Under this pressure to finish so much, time agreements are often made more frequently to speed up the process.

In the modern Senate, deadlines such as the end of the fiscal year or large important expiring provisions, such as the highway bill or the Federal Aviation Authority reauthorization, determine much of the broader schedule. The preexisting, known deadlines indicate to the majority which weeks they must keep open for deadline-driven items and which they can fill with their own message bills (bills that are designed to draw a contrast between the political parties and are not necessarily expected to advance) or more focused bills (dealing with very specific issues such as toxic chemical safety or immigration reform that have no specific deadline but are of interest to the chamber). Once a decision is made about what will be on the floor for a given week, the days of the week have a relatively predictable flow. Keep this flow in mind as you evaluate the political context of what is happening on the floor, because it can often tell you what pressure points are coming.

In an average Senate week, the floor opens on Monday afternoon, often with a bed-check vote (similar to that in the House, see p. 13), used to get the machinery of the Senate up and running for the week. Typically, this occurs at 5:30 p.m. and often is a noncontroversial vote such as a nomination, an amendment, or a procedural vote that eases members and staff into the week before the big discussions begin on Tuesday (although when things are busy, the Monday votes can also be quite substantive). Mondays also allow the leadership teams to meet and make early plans for the week.

On Tuesday, the Senate tends to open with an hour for general debate, called morning business, where senators can discuss any topic. Then the Senate turns to consideration of the business of the week. On Tuesdays the floor typically recesses from 12:30 to 2:15 p.m. to allow for the weekly party caucus luncheons. At these luncheons the parties decide how they want to deal with the week's scheduled activities: Will there be cooperation? What does the minority seek in return for cooperating with the majority? What do majority members need in order to further the business at hand? If there is not enough will to pass a bill or adopt a motion to proceed, how will failure play out? During this time messaging decisions may also be discussed by both parties. For example, the individual parties may discuss what themes will be emphasized throughout the week.

From this point onward through the remainder of the week, Senate watchers can see how the discourse between the parties, or between active members on an issue, will play out. By Tuesday afternoon it will often be more clear if a bill can move forward. If the legislative priority of the week is in good health—that is, it is moving along productively with little obstruction—work will be done to push ahead, round out negotiations, and deal with whatever is needed in terms of amendment votes or debate to pass the bill by Thursday afternoon, or to at least set a path to finish the bill. But if it appears the will is lacking to successfully move whatever bill is on the floor—whether because of bad timing, unrelated (but often timely and also important) political fights, obstruction by an energetic minority with issues surrounding the bill, an issue not ripe enough to garner the votes, or for some other reason—floor time will end up being used in discussion, morning business, or procedural votes such as cloture, and messaging so the caucuses can explain why a bill failed and articulate who or what they think is to blame. Note that this is often due to substantive policy disagreements or fighting for amendment slots, and slowing down a bill is often a means of expressing that and encouraging a negotiation. This is not to be taken as process for its own sake; these are tools and part of the way the senators communicate with each other, build pressure for deals, and create discourse for issues they care about.

Occasionally it takes longer for more pressure to build and indicate how a bill may go. For example, the caucuses may come out of their Tuesday lunches hoping to try to find a path but unsure what it may be, and a bill may look like it will fail. So sometimes a bill appears to be going poorly, but after a filing to invoke cloture and thus limit debate, there can potentially be focus and members are able to make a deal or find a path forward; for example, an agreement may come together that allows for an amendment or promise for consideration of a bill at a future time, or something else that helps increase support for the bill at hand, or at least for the process of its moving forward. Various rules are used to create pressure points. This is a crucial dynamic to watch in the Senate. Often, new staff will read the rules and understandably want to apply them in pure form, but the Senate rules are rarely used in their pure form—rules are used to create pressure points that often bring about a shift to deals or time agreements. Similarly, just because a particular procedural maneuver is possible does not

mean it is politically advisable. For example, there may
be available amendment slots that a member wants to
use for an amendment they like but that may be politically charged; they have to ask themselves, "What will
the chairman or ranking member managing the bill
think, what will the leaderships think, would offering
such an amendment potentially hurt a bipartisan bill?"
Some may still decide it is worth it to offer, but these are
important considerations. Similarly, at any given time
there are usually several smaller often unnoticed motions available to be made that can slow progress, but
they cannot be used in a vacuum. Everything in the
Senate is action and reaction. And when gauging if
something is worth doing or advisable or can help achieve
a certain goal, it must also be viewed in that give-and-
take context as well. Just because something is possible
on the floor does not necessarily make it advisable in
terms of floor dynamics. The rules must be understood in
the context of the surrounding pressures and the political
reality of any given Senate day, bill, or event.

This flow day by day is another contrast with the
House, where the majority steers the process through
the House Rules Committee. In the Senate all members can participate in the weekly or daily setting of
debate parameters, often ultimately represented by negotiations between the two parties' leadership.

Wednesday is often the day when the meat of the
week's negotiations takes place if a bill is going well. It
is also a busy day generally as it is a very active committee hearing day (Tuesday and Thursday morning are as
well). Wednesday is often when substantive conversations take place about amendments being considered or

other important matters. If things are not moving, the day is often used to file cloture in order to help build pressure and force decisions both within one caucus and between the caucuses. A few members may need to decide whether they can make a deal, or it may be that one party cannot be satisfied and will decide to vote against cloture, or there is a last-minute successful time agreement to pass the bill (that is, a pathway is found using consent and deal making to outline a path to the finish). In any case, sometimes it takes a cloture filing to force those decisions; otherwise, debate can continue endlessly. For example, when Congress passed legislation relating to Puerto Rico to which there was opposition, cloture was filed and invoked to move forward. During the thirty hours of post-cloture debate, a time agreement was reached to yield back fifteen of the possible thirty hours in exchange for a series of votes. Through this deal, supporters of the bill gained clarity on a timeline-driven bill, and opponents were able to demonstrate their priorities through the agreed voting series. You may wonder why some of these decisions cannot be made earlier in the bill process: Why should cloture be needed to force focus? The answer is a mix of human nature and politics. Often, pressure has to build to make tough decisions or to make negotiations feasible. Also, recall that the members have several responsibilities throughout the week. Other than the bill managers and leaders, it may be that most members are focused on committee work or other matters and do not shift their attention to the flow of floor work until told, "Action is really closing down on this bill!" Cloture can often force this refocus of attention.

On Thursday, the rubber hits the road—senators must decide whether or not a deal is possible. If the end is in sight to pass a bill, they can make time agreements that move votes to Thursday afternoon so that senators can return to their states and constituents for Friday and beyond.

Usually in any given week one or two major issues drive events on the Senate floor. These issues may be from one of two calendars, the executive calendar and the legislative calendar. They may be driven by both calendars. On the executive calendar are treaties and nominations that have been reported from committees to the floor; it is the constitutionally listed prerogative of the Senate to give advice and consent to the executive branch on these items. On the legislative calendar are a variety of legislative tools and vehicles. Both calendars also sometimes list holds—public notices of a senator's objection to an item moving forward. Both calendars also include any outstanding consent agreements. Both calendars contain a wealth of information regarding the business of the Senate, such as the status of appropriations bills, committee assignments, the date when an item was reported to the calendar, and a listing of the three Senate classes—representing the group of senators to stand for election at the same time (one-third of the senators every two years). Every so often, the Senate session will go into Friday or through the weekend. This is often due to an urgent matter being considered, or can also be due to dramatic circumstances. For example, during consideration of the Affordable Care Act the Senate was in continuous session and during the "shutdown" of 2013 Congress worked continuously in Washington until a solution was found.

TYPES OF BILLS

The legislative process, year, month, and week have their own cycle. What is being described in pieces is largely those cycles in more detail—the rules and then the negotiations. As part of that, much in the Senate is described as "generally" instead of "always" because there are exceptions to everything. Like in the House, relatively few individuals understand the entirety of the rules and their attending texts and precedents, and so members and staff are advised by the floor staffs representing the majority and minority parties and by the Senate parliamentarians, especially on more complex or exceptional maneuvers. However, there are some recurring terms that are helpful in this review of the legislative process. The key floor staffs that run hotlines and conduct many of the cross-party floor negotiations are based in the cloakrooms that each party has, which are located directly off the Senate floor. These staffs advise the leaderships, and also the floor managers. When a particular bill is being considered, the chairman and ranking member of the committee that has jurisdiction over the bill become the floor managers, and, along with other members and the leaders, manage the process of using the rules and negotiations to move a bill through the floor process. That process could include amendments, cloture or time agreements, success or failure. As you read through the different pieces, it is common to experience the individual parts making more sense at the end, once they all fit together.

Politically and practically, the legislative items listed in the legislative calendar fall into three general (though not technical) categories:

Boutique bills are issue-specific bills that focus on particular issues such as cyber security or veterans' affairs and are usually driven by one or a few major champions. Their making it as far as the calendar is often a result of enjoying bipartisan support.

Deadline-driven bills are bills related to issues that must be addressed by a certain date such as the debt limit, funding the government, or the expiration of programs such as the Highway Trust Fund. Until relatively recently, these types of bills were often helped to the finish by a mechanism of congressionally directed spending or projects called "earmarks," whereby members would advocate for and then point to specific resources coming to their state. Earmark-like moves are still sometimes seen, but the practice in general ended in 2010. These big deadline-driven, must-pass bills are now more driven by political pressure and top-level negotiations and messaging between the House, the Senate, and the White House.

Messaging bills are fairly common and could be said to be born to fail—that is, their real purpose is not necessarily to become the law of the land. Instead, they are designed to send a message to the public about issues that distinguish the political parties from each other, or they create difficult or otherwise politically advantageous votes. Often these bills are given names that sound very direct in purpose, partisan or confrontational. These bills often fail to achieve the consensus they need to be debated, so the majority leader files cloture on the motion to proceed, and then the cloture vote often fails. To illustrate the importance of time for the majority party, even in such a case almost a week can be spent introducing and trying to debate these messaging bills.

TAKING VOTES

The Senate has different ways of actually taking votes. Generally, senators vote in person by saying "yea" or "nay." The most common types of votes taken are the voice vote and the roll call vote. Different types of motions also determine the nuts and bolts of voting, some motions requiring a different process and a different proportion of votes than do others.

Roll call. Often, voting in the Senate is done by roll call. A roll-call vote in the Senate usually takes about twenty minutes. The vote closes at the discretion of the majority leader so sometimes votes go longer than the usual fifteen to twenty minutes. Leaving a vote open longer than anticipated may be used as an opportunity to negotiate or sway the votes of undecided or opposing senators.

Voice vote. An informal poll of the Senate by voice, often used for noncontroversial items where a few members wish to vote no but it is not worth the full Senate's voting by roll call. The chair (a member of the majority who presides over the Senate when it is in session) asks who votes yea and who votes nay, and each group shouts its response. The louder group wins the voice vote. Voice votes are generally used when the result is widely known. If the result isn't clear, a roll call vote can be requested by any senator with a sufficient second.

Vote by division. This requires standing, being counted, and then sitting, and is sometimes used for voting on treaties.

WORKING THROUGH THE PROCESS
AND THE ROLE OF THE MAJORITY

Certain bills have a better chance of surviving the process on the Senate floor. Often bills that are destined for success are must-pass and come to the floor pre-negotiated and pre-whipped, as this also means they may not take as much time. Boutique bills may survive because the parties are motivated to negotiate within their memberships to move forward on a narrow subject and the bill is small in scope and impact, or it has enough items riding with it that it enjoys a broad coalition, or it is timely. Other bills with a good prognosis for survival include popular bills on timely topics without much opposition (such bills are said to be ripe); bills with strong and bipartisan coalitions or media support; bills on which interested senators have spent months or years negotiating; bills that have been through a thorough process, and senators feel that their rights have been respected and so are satisfied with the amount of debate the bill has received.

Majority Rule Versus Consent

Although unanimous consent is very important on the Senate floor and minority rights are a hallmark of Senate dynamics, the majority party has a significant advantage. The majority customarily has control over the Senate floor and sets the agenda. This power is maintained in four primary ways:

1. A member of the majority always presides over the Senate when it is in session. The presiding officer

serves as a temporary president of the Senate, also called the chair.

2. The majority has a majority of votes in the chamber so it can marshal votes needed for maneuvers such as tabling an amendment or force attempts to an adjournment.

3. The majority assigns committee chairmanships and thus controls committee agendas.

4. The majority leader or majority bill manager has priority recognition, which means that he or she will be called on first if more than one senator is seeking to speak on the floor. Having recognition over all other senators is extremely important for controlling the floor—arguably priority recognition is the majority party's most significant power.

Some commonly used tools for managing the floor include:

* sending the Senate into a quorum call by asking the clerk to slowly read the roll;

* requiring unanimous consent or a vote to come out of the quorum call so that a senator can speak;

* filling the amendment tree (a procedural tool to limit the changes to a bill and limit what votes are possible without consent);

* moving to a certain bill by making a motion to proceed or to a nomination; or

* speaking or asking consents ahead of others who may seek to obstruct or create a surprise on the floor.

With these tools, the majority can set the agenda and can control the general flow of floor action. Unlike in the House, however, the majority party cannot control the clock because the Senate is an institution designed for unfettered debate, where each of the senators can block expedited action. All 100 senators have certain rights that empower them on the floor and give them at least some negotiating leverage with the majority leader or bill managers to attempt to get what they want. Absent consent there are three options: gridlock, move on to other business, or forge ahead by attempting cloture.

Objecting to the Senate's moving forward on consideration of a bill or nomination is known as filibustering. A filibuster obstructs progress on an item, for any reason, related or unrelated. It occurs when at least one member wants to continue debate and block conclusion or consideration of an item. However, the term "filibuster" has come to mean for many any objection or threat to moving a bill, and the majority leader will often file for cloture just to bring conclusion one way or another or to create a baseline timeline so that negotiations can commence from there on a time agreement. In the Senate, the rights of each senator are so valued that their objections often can even be registered remotely, without their necessarily having to appear on the floor.

Germaneness

An additional consideration of Senate dynamics is germaneness. In the House, typically amendments contemplated must be germane to the subject of the bill being considered. In the Senate, under the principle of unfettered debate, generally there is no requirement for germaneness. As a starting point, the Senate amendment process is meant to be fairly open. This means that unrelated matters can often be offered as amendment to bills on the floor, and amendments that expand the scope of a bill are allowed.

Yet, germaneness is still relevant under certain scenarios and it always can affect negotiations of amendment consent agreements. If cloture is invoked and debate on a bill is ending without consent to protect non-germane amendments, a germaneness requirement is applied, and amendments must be related to the bill's subject and not expand its scope. However, this can be altered by agreements that can set up germaneness or relative requirements for amendments even pre-cloture. Incentives for such negotiations post-cloture tends to decline as a bill has shown it already has the ability to move forward. Generally speaking, changes made by germane amendments are looked on more favorably than non-germane amendments, but either can be accomplished.

Appropriations bills and budget resolutions are subject to different germaneness standards than other bills. For example, amendments to appropriations bills may not add authorizing language to appropriations bills, and budget amendments are impacted by the Byrd Rule, which governs budget impact measurements and entitlements. This process in and of itself is quite complex, and there are plenty of resources publicly available to dive deeper, including budget.senate.gov.

Committees

Committees are another important factor in the health of a bill or an issue and its prognosis for survival on the floor. Senate committees are an important aspect of the Senate's functioning. It is in committees where many relationships are formed, where senators become issue experts, and where the early or most meaty part of the negotiations on a bill may take place. Even with a healthy committee process, however, there are no guarantees for a bill on the floor. Even if a bill comes out of committee with a lot of support, that still means that only about thirty senators have had direct access to it—although others may have had indirect access. Savvy members may get language included in the bill even if they are not on the committee of jurisdiction, and smart bill sponsors will enable just that kind of input to give as many members as possible some reason to support the bill as it moves through the process.

When the bill is just out of committee, the senators not on the committee may not be as invested in the subject or the issue as the committee members, and some members may seek to use a moving vehicle for purposes other than the bill's subject matter. When that happens, often the leadership must be involved with the bill managers to determine if there is a path forward, even if adding an external matter (perhaps through an amendment) must be considered. Gaining the support of off-committee senators is also further motivation for floor managers to push for so-called floor amendments to a bill, even if the amendments are not relevant to the bill's original intent. Floor amendments can also help when bill managers determine that something is best negotiated by the full Senate instead of in committee. In their markups committee chairs or ranking committee members may often promise a floor process instead of committee process on particularly difficult subjects.

Thus, a bill's prognosis for smooth movement through the Senate process is a question as much of politics as of the substance of the bill.

Amendments and the Amendment Tree

Amendments also play an important role in the legislative process. They are often discussed on the floor but are one of the most complicated tools. An amendment is the tool through which individual senators can make changes to proposed legislation. This is true in theory— in theory, a senator can offer an amendment to any bill. However, there are procedural steps to this process, and in practice it can be much more limited or complicated. Members often file amendments to a bill, meaning that they have sent the amendment to the floor to be tracked and posted to a public amendment tracking system. It does not mean that the amendment is pending to the bill. Offering an amendment to a bill, to make it actually pending business, or offering an amendment to an amendment that is already pending to the bill (called an amendment in the second degree) can be difficult or easy depending on cooperation levels and requires its own strategy.

Getting an amendment considered requires cooperation from the majority. To understand the amendment process one must understand the "amendment tree." This is a colloquial term for the amendment slots available on a legislative vehicle. The majority leader can use a procedural tool known as "filling the tree," which means filling up all of the existing amendment slots on a bill so that it takes consent for anyone else to offer any amendments, unless one of the filler amendments can be tabled—a common political maneuver—but even then the majority leader has priority recognition, so it tends to be symbolic. Think of a bill that has been put on the floor as a tree trunk. In a basic amendment tree, on the right side of the tree trunk is a branch, and that branch is the first-degree amendment slot. That branch represents the first amendment added to the bill. Attached to that branch is a twig, which is the second-degree amendment slot. On the left side of the tree is a branch called a motion to recommit the bill, and that has a first-degree amendment, meaning a motion to send a bill back to committee for the purpose of adding a specific amendment. Attached to that branch is a twig that is a second-degree amendment to the first-degree amendment.

There are several permutations of this basic structure. The most common permutation is a substitute tree, on which the right-side branch is a total replacement for the tree trunk, and has its own first-degree and second-degree twigs. In addition, there is a little extra branch on the right side that amends the original language and has its own twig as a second-degree slot (see samples in appendix D).

If the majority leader does not want to have an amendment process, he or she will use the privilege of priority recognition to fill the tree before any other senator has the opportunity to insert other amendments. It is a move often used when time is of the essence, for example, when the government must be funded or the debt limit increased, and there is no time for lengthy debate on an amendment. Or it can be used toward the end of an amendment process to signal that the Senate should be ready to finish a bill. Or it can be threatened but not used, as everyone is aware that the majority has the ability to fill a tree and keep it full. Although that maneuver is rare, the knowledge that it is possible often structures the background of negotiations over floor paths and amendments.

In addition, the majority leader often fills the slots on the amendment tree to avoid poison pill amendments— amendments that are likely to either halt consent agreements and slow progress on the bill, or to make it more difficult to get the bill passed or that could force an otherwise favored bill to fail or face a veto threat. This maneuver has been used differently in different eras of Congress and by different leaders, but the possibility is always a part of Senate dynamics.

What increases an amendment's chances of being considered? Often senators are advised to offer their amendments early in the process of consideration of a bill, before things potentially slow down or freeze as a bill heads to completion or failure. They are encouraged to begin discussing their amendment with the bill managers and leadership as early as possible, build support coalitions, and draft the amendment to be germane to the bill so that even without consent, if cloture is invoked on the bill, the amendment can get a vote. There are many traps in those scenarios, but that is the magic and mystery of the Senate floor. Because of the powers of all 100 senators, it is rarely safe for senators to bet on being able to wage a full battle for an amendment on the floor alone. A senator must start early—get in a committee mark, make it a committee amendment where only a majority of the committee is needed, be early in a leadership negotiation if it is a must-pass bill, or a last-resort fight in conference. Waging a floor fight is generally thought of as a last resort for a bill or can be used for political purposes.

The majority leader is not the only one using amendments to maneuver in the Senate. There are many reasons for a senator to file an amendment—actually pending it to a bill is just one of them. A senator may want to build pressure for an issue, threaten to offer an amendment to get something from a chairman or a leader, want to send a signal on an issue he or she will work on in the future, or, explore a new idea, among other reasons. Once again, context matters a lot and amendment filings should be evaluated through that lens. As with everything in the Senate, is it extremely important to consider looking beyond the official rules.

A sample   When the Senate considered a comprehensive immigration reform bill, the pathway of the bill covered many of the basic procedural moves covered above.

After much negotiation, a bill was introduced and sent to the judiciary committee for hearings and markup. When it came to the floor, a "first-degree blocker" amendment was offered—an uncontroversial amendment, usually offered by a floor manager—to fill the first amendment slot, so that the bill's sponsors control it and it takes some cooperation or maneuvering for other amendments to be made pending. On the floor, several other amendments were offered with cooperation, some were considered with time agreements (consent), but several were still pending when a large negotiation took place over adding further border provisions to the text that had moved the bill from introduction, through committee, and to the floor. But this was the last step in securing the votes for cloture and passage. A new substitute amendment had to be offered and cloture filed on that substitute amendment and on the underlying bill. When that happens, pending amendments are no longer drafted correctly because they reference text that no longer exists, and as such fall away. Some of the original amendment sponsors may be satisfied in other ways—while some others lost in an overall larger process, designed to move a large legislative vehicle that had pieces of many senators' bills, amendments, and ideas.

GETTING A BILL TO THE FLOOR

Items that are considered in the Senate can originate in multiple ways: a senator can introduce a bill or resolution, or a House-passed bill or joint resolution may be received in the Senate from the House, or a previously introduced bill may be amended with new material. (Note that regular resolutions are single-chamber, so an S.Res. is considered and adopted only in the Senate, and an H.Res. is considered only in the House. This is in contrast to other types of resolutions.) Treaties and nominations for public office arrive in the Senate from the executive branch. There are seven main ways to get a bill to the floor of the Senate:

1. The standard committee process
2. The Senate's "Rule 14" procedure to bypass committees and place an item directly on the calendar

3. Bills from the House of Representatives (known as HR vehicles)

4. A unanimous consent or a hotline process

5. Conferences/House messages (privileged vehicles/other special vehicles)

6. The substitution of a new text in a preexisting bill vehicle

7. An amendment to a moving vehicle/bill package

The Standard Committee Process

The standard committee process, also referred to as regular order, is the best-known way for a bill to travel the path to becoming a law. Typically, a senator files a bill on the Senate floor, at which point the Senate parliamentarian's office assigns it to a committee of jurisdiction. This process almost mirrors the process of the House except that in the Senate there is generally only one committee of jurisdiction, called single referral, rather than the possibility of referral to multiple committees or consecutive referrals, as in the House. In rare exceptions, with cooperation, a bill may be considered by more than one committee, but it requires special requests and action.

Senators often are mindful of which committee they think their bill may be referred to. If they think they can, they may attempt to tweak the draft language of their bill to steer it toward a committee that will view it more favorably. A variety of factors may make some committees friendlier than others, but most often the main consideration is the membership of the committee. But the potential of such gamesmanship by any single senator may be limited because committees have fairly clearly defined jurisdictions over broad topics and will see most bills falling under their defined jurisdictions. For example, the Finance Committee has jurisdiction over trade issues, so typically anything impacting trade will go to that committee, regardless of how the bill is worded.

Once referred to committee, a bill may sit there indefinitely, or the committee may hold hearings on it. A hearing is a type of oversight or study of an issue. After hearings the bill may still die in committee, or it may get a markup and be reported out. A markup is when the committee actually considers and votes on whether to send legislation or nominations to the full Senate for further discussion, called "reporting out." When a bill is marked up and reported out, it is put on the legislative calendar after one "hold over" day; similarly, nominations and treaties are reported to the executive calendar. The majority leader can then choose whether or not to make a motion to proceed to that item at some time during the Congress. At any point during this process a bill can be moved by unanimous consent, or a bill might sit on the calendar until the end of a Congress, at which point it expires and may be reintroduced in another Congress.

The Rule 14 Process

Rule 14 is shorthand for a mechanism whereby matters are quickly moved to the calendar for potential consideration. Though Rule 14 is technically a standing rule that covers various aspects of bill introduction and consideration, the term "Rule 14" is colloquially used to mean this fast-track process. The process takes three legislative days, and specific steps are required, as follows:

On day 1, a senator requests the first reading of a bill directly to the calendar. The first read is generally not actually a word-for-word reading of the whole bill. Instead, the senator asks for unanimous consent to consider the bill as read, so that the Senate can move on to other business. The text will appear in the record as read word for word, but floor time has not been used for a real reading. On day 2, the bill is due for its second reading, and a similar process is followed. On day 3, the bill is added to the Senate legislative calendar, so that a motion to proceed may be made to it, if that is the desired path. (Often, however, bills are read to the calendar and stay there indefinitely.) This entire process can be truncated by unanimous consent that the bill will be read to the calendar immediately, and sometimes the motion to proceed is adopted without delay. But if any member has a reason to delay proceedings, he or she might at any time object to a consent request and force the bill to be read verbatim or added to the calendar and moved to by the book, which requires several days and cloture.

The Rule 14 process is used for a variety of reasons. Although the process does technically circumvent committees, it does not mean a committee has not been involved in the text or process, which is why context is so important. For example, a deal that has been made at the last minute might need to be put on the calendar quickly. Or it might be a bill that was altered so substantially in the committee process that it is easier to simply start with a clean new bill that incorporates all of the changes rather than present a messy hodgepodge of original language and amendments. Another factor is that time is often a worry for the majority leader, who must accommodate legislation and nominations. To try to avoid some common delay opportunities by any opposition, the majority leader may choose to Rule 14 a bill to avoid having to debate controversial committee amendments on the floor. Invoking Rule 14 might also be more politically motivated: perhaps the chairman of the committee of jurisdiction is unfriendly to the bill but the majority leadership looks on it positively. Or it may be a bill that only a small minority of the Senate have interest in and they want to show some advancement. A majority leader may also Rule 14 a bill for pure management reasons, such as a House revenue vehicle that may be needed quickly during a deadline-driven negotiation in order to fund the government or extend tax provisions; such a vehicle, independent of its substance, is helpful to have on the calendar. In general, Rule 14 can be used to expedite getting something to the floor when necessary or desired.

HR Vehicle

Some bills come to the Senate from the House of Representatives (HR bills), and these can be held at the desk, meaning they are on hold until a decision can be made about their fate. It will be decided whether the bill can be passed quickly with consent, Rule 14'd to the calendar, or sent to committee. House bills are likely to be held at the desk or Rule 14'd if they cover some politically charged or interesting topic such as the Affordable Care Act or if the bill has revenue implications and needs to be on the Senate calendar in a timely fashion when the Senate has to work on revenue, appropriations, and tax issues. If not,

HR bills are often referred to the committee that has the appropriate jurisdiction.

Consent, or "Hotlining"

Another way a bill may reach the Senate floor is consent. At any point in the legislative process, an item can be hotlined, which means that the majority leader (via the floor staff) sends a message directly to all 100 Senate offices (by email and phone) saying, "The majority leader would like to pass or adopt this. If you disagree with that, please let the floor staff know." This is called "running a hotline" (see appendix A). If no senator objects, the item will pass, the nomination confirmed, or the time agreement entered. If a senator objects with "a hold," the item cannot pass without further action, negotiation, or floor time. A hold is a way for senators to object and are usually secret. Hotlines cover the array of Senate happenings. The hotline process is used constantly in the Senate at every stage of consideration of a bill, but it is used most commonly for items that have come from committee, or in order to secure time agreements to consider bills on the floor, or to speed along commemorative resolutions or other such narrowly focused, usually bipartisan, items.

A technical note on hotlines: each party has a "cloakroom," a space that is connected to the Senate floor (beautifully described in Robert Caro's classic *The Master of the Senate.* Many discussions and negotiations, and the running of hotlines to assess whether consent agreements are possible, happen in these nerve centers of each caucus. These spaces are also used for negotiating both among a party's own members and across parties, managing the hotline process, tracking senator attendance, and helping members get up to speed on what is happening on the floor at any given point. The cloak-rooms are also where the core floor staff sit and where the actual emails and calls that are the "hotline requests" are drafted and sent. The majority sends hotlines to their side, and the minority sends hotlines to their side, from their respective cloakrooms. If a hotline has cleared, it means both parties have run it. There is no set duration for a hotline; some sent in urgent circumstances are only out for ten minutes before being locked in, while some are pending for weeks before being settled. It depends on the topic, the circumstance, and how much pressure there is to move something along, versus if there is any passionate opposition or not, and if there is a negotiated path possi-ble or not. Since so much business is conducted through the hotline system, there are many permutations of how things are sent, asked, and negotiated this way. Also of note is that just because a hotline is requested by one party, a member, or committee, it does not mean the hot-line will necessarily run on both sides of Senate.

The hotline system can also be used to uncover prob-lems or grievances with a given legislative item and thus help move negotiations along. Sometimes both a hotline and passage of a bill will occur in one day. Sometimes a hotline runs and the bill does not pass at all because of holds, or it passes, but only after weeks or months of fol-low-up negotiations, or with an agreement for some set amount of debate time or a set list of amendments.

The hotline system, which can speed things up dra-matically, is essential to the Senate in order to clear a lot of business since floor time is scarce. The importance of time for unfettered debate in the Senate cannot be em-phasized enough. Thus, items that can use unanimous consent or the hotline process to move forward tend to have the best luck.

Privileged or Other Special Vehicles: Conferences, House Messages, Statutory Items

Some legislative vehicles are termed "privileged" because they are treated with some fast-tracking on the Senate floor. The two most-used forms are conference reports and House messages (also called the "ping-pong"). Both are tools used to settle differences between the House and Senate on legislation and ensure that each chamber ultimately passes the same actual bill text to be sent to the president. The idea of privilege comes from the fact that a bill has already had its time on the Senate floor, been debated (either on the floor or behind the scenes ahead of a consent agreement), and thus does not need to be greatly delayed or given extended debate time; a conference report or House message can come to the floor without the need to debate a motion to proceed. The Senate can speed to consideration of the item itself, subject to only one cloture petition if needed.

Being included in a conference report is another way for a bill to reach the floor. The report may be subject to a point-of-order vote on the floor, which challenges the bill's inclusion as a new matter. Note that even the process of sending legislation to conference is faster than dealing with usual legislation, as it has a truncated cloture debate time (two hours), if cloture is even needed.

Another type of privileged vehicle is a message that has been ping-ponged between the House and Senate. In this scenario, a matter is essentially negotiated between the two chambers' floors by amending a bill and sending it back and forth. In addition to the main substance of the bill, sometimes these vehicles are saved on the calendar and used at a later time to move unrelated matters quickly.

There are some special vehicles that have fast-track processes for coming to the Senate floor, so they are not necessarily privileged but they have many of the same characteristics in that they are often not amendable or have limited amendment opportunities, as well as have the ability to move faster than normal legislation. For example, resolutions of disapproval under the Congressional Review Act are subject to majority thresholds for motions to proceed to adoption with only up to ten hours of debate, equally divided between opponents and proponents. Another example is the legislation used to waive the military service break years for the nomination of General James Mattis for secretary of defense in 2017; this legislation was designed by statute to have limited debate and a single sixty-vote threshold passage vote. A third example is the legislation used to review the Iran nuclear deal; this legislation has its own process as designed by statute. And the fourth example, mentioned elsewhere, is the budget and reconciliation process, also operating under different-than-usual rules.

Substituting a New Text, and Amendment
to a Moving Vehicle, Bill Packages

In the modern Senate, moving large bills with many amendments is less common but still does happen with some frequency. It may be that the text of a bill can be included in a larger agreement, and all of the new text is read into a bill that has been sitting on the calendar for a long time. For example, a joint resolution regarding sanctions on Myanmar (Burma) was used to pass a large spending bill; a substitute amendment was used to alter the original text. Or a bill could be drafted as an amendment and added to another bill—on a related subject or not—that is already moving. For example, an amendment to expand the right to carry guns on Amtrak trains was considered and passed on a bill to reform credit card practices. Often defense-related bills are turned into amendments and added to the annual defense authorization bill when it moves on the floor. Another way to move a bill is to combine several related bills or amendments to form a larger bill with a single theme. This can help all of the smaller bills within the larger one pass with less overall floor time used.

PROCEDURAL TOOLS IN THE SENATE

The role of rules in the Senate varies a bit from the House in that they are designed to provide a baseline for majority and minority activity, but often result in a fluid negotiation. While the House builds on and sets new rules every two years, changes to the rules in the Senate are more rare and in some ways difficult to make. In the House, the Rules Committee can waive rules to favor the majority. In contrast to this, the Senate procedures generally apply unless they have been explicitly changed by a two-thirds vote, statute, or negotiation, or a new precedent has been set. Over time rules have been updated or changed, in their own right or as a result of precedent changes (which may happen with the use of the "nuclear option"); such changes have often been years in the making.

The rules are used to create pressure points and drive momentum, helping a majority advance its agenda while preserving minority rights. These tools each have their own role to play throughout the life cycle of the floor. Committees, too, often have rules that impact how bills or nominations may move or customs that impact the hotline process. The committees are able to set more of their own norms and generally remain quite constant, compared to the House, which changes more frequently.

The Senate majority has some distinctive tools to help manage the floor and set the agenda for a given Congress, but any political minority, a handful of disgruntled senators, or perhaps even a single senator, has great resources to impact or disrupt the agenda and goings-on on the floor—different kinds of motions, resolutions, and votes. Most of these tools involve the potential for virtually endless debate, which in turn affects how quickly the majority is allowed to advance its goals or is prevented from doing so. The Senate rules favor the idea that debate is important for both majority and minority rights and can potentially improve outcomes. Also, there are only 100 senators, and time and rhetoric are the coin of the realm. Unanimous consents and artful deal making can accomplish almost anything. When there are no deals to be made or a senator decides to obstruct with the full potential of the toolbox of tactics, work can be brought to a halt.

A number of procedural tools are used in the Senate, often in ways that a new observer may find curious. To understand the nuances of the tools' deployment one must study and evaluate their use in context: How popular is the bill on the floor? What are the committee dynamics? What are the caucus dynamics? Is there a deadline?

Common Moves and Terms

Many types of motions, votes, vehicles, and terms are used on the Senate floor, but just a handful are used on a regular basis (remember the 80-20 rule), and in this section we provide readers with a ready reference to these most common moves. When an item is debatable, it generally means that it may be subject to cloture, unless there is cooperation or the Senate is already post-cloture.

Motion to proceed   In the Senate, it can take debate to even begin considering a matter. Thus, a senator makes a motion to proceed in order to move to a vehicle. That vehicle generally has to be on the legislative calendar in order for the motion to proceed to be made. The motion is generally debatable and thus can require a cloture motion if there is not consent to move to a bill—that is, not consent to adopt the motion to proceed by consent, or by an immediate roll call or voice vote. That means it is subject to a majority if there is cooperation or to a cloture threshold (three-fifths of the Senate, that is sixty) if cloture is needed.

In the Senate, the majority party controls the floor, meaning that the majority leader typically decides what the floor agenda will be and brings bills to the floor for consideration. He or she will try to adopt a motion to proceed via unanimous consent. If that is not possible, he or she will file a motion to proceed to consider the bill—motion to proceed, for short—and often have to file cloture on that motion to proceed. Some alternative routes to adopting a motion to proceed requiring bipartisan cooperation and amendments have been created but have not yet been used. Motions to proceed are occasionally the only aspect of a bill that gets debated. Sometimes the Senate rejects a motion to proceed by voting down invoking cloture to end debate on that motion and the majority must move on to something else. But let's suppose the motion to proceed is adopted. In this case, the bill is the pending business of the floor. Sometimes a new motion to proceed will be made pending as a defensive measure by the majority. It can be a technicality that is used to prevent the minority or a member of the majority from hijacking floor time for other aims. If no motion is pending while a bill is being considered and a senator wants to move to something else but the leadership disagrees, the senator can file a motion to bring up something else. By having a motion already pending, floor leaders can prevent something surprising from being brought up instead. The leadership also often uses this tactic to indicate to the public what legislative item is expected up next on the floor, after whatever is being currently considered.

An example will help illustrate how this works. The Senate had adopted a motion to proceed to a bill and has thus started debating that bill. The moment the motion to proceed was adopted, that slot in the agenda opened up and was available during debate on the legislation. To prevent mischief or surprise, sometimes the majority leader will fill the slot with a motion to proceed to another bill. So it may look as though the pending business was the pending motion to proceed, while it is actually the business being debated. It can be confusing. When the Senate is debating a motion to proceed, you have to pay attention to see if that is the actual business or if something else is the underlying business. Note that if the second motion to proceed is not acted on, it expires at the end of the day and has to be renewed, if needed, the following day. Also note that this is not an issue if the Senate is post-cloture (that is, if cloture has been invoked and the Senate is burning up to thirty hours of post-cloture time).

Motions to proceed are a frequent topic of discussion about potential changes to the Senate rules. Some senators do not want a minority to be able to block going to direct debate on some bills, especially appropriations bills, so there is some debate about changing the Senate rules to make the motion to proceed non-debatable, which means it would not be subject to cloture, not subject to a supermajority standard, and not subject to extended debates. But so far, this has been only under discussion, among the many other popular discussion points of Senate procedure. And of note, more often than not, motions to proceed are adopted by consent as items clear in the hotline and consent process.

"The wrap up"   At the end of most days, the two cloakrooms will manage a "wrap up"—which is an agreement about when the Senate will adjourn for the evening, setting up the start of the next day, and passing or adopting any business that has been cleared by both parties through the hotline process. When something has "cleared in wrap up," this generally means that it was able to pass by agreement with consent or a voice vote and will happen in the end-of-day process. The "wrap up" refers to when a member of the majority party reads through the procedural items needed to adjourn the Senate for the night, brings it in the next day, and adopts/passes/confirms whatever has been cleared

to move by consent. Wrap ups can be found in the *Congressional Record* and occur on most days.

Motion to table   This is a non-debatable motion that disposes of an issue to be dealt with another day or maybe in another way. It is often used by the majority to shelve amendments or motions it is not happy with. A motion to table is subject to a majority threshold of those present and voting, and "not debatable" means that the motion can be made and then a vote happens immediately (as opposed to when cloture has to be filed first).

Motion to recess the Senate   A "call to recess the Senate" is almost never voted on, but you may see the Senate recess "subject to the Call of the Chair." This is a way to pause the action for a member briefing or joint session, or when there is a long pause between speakers, and the presiding officer needs to move around, without having the Senate actually end the session day.

Motion to adjourn   This is a motion to adjourn the Senate. It can trump all other motions. A motion to adjourn the Senate is the highest form of a motion and is almost always in order if made (that means it can be made pending). The Senate almost never votes on the motion to adjourn and usually plans to adjourn by consent. Nightly adjournments or adjournment with a deal are very common when the Senate is transitioning to a recess/district work period. This is used to set up "pro forma" dates during which the Senate briefly meets during a recess time to break up recess days and prevent recess appointments, which can only occur during a formal adjournment. As motions to adjourn are generally adopted by consent, so are adjournment resolutions. The resolutions are what set up the "recess" or "district work periods." When an adjournment resolution is not adopted, pro forma sessions must occur. During these pro forma sessions, no business is conducted, and it is the Senate convening for a few minutes every three days to only technically not be in adjournment. Each chamber may formally adjourn or have pro forma sessions on their own without impacting the other. At the end of a Congress, there is a special type of adjournment called "sine die," the executive and legislative calendars clear, and the new Congress begins on January 3 at noon of every odd-numbered year.

Live quorum/motion to instruct   In theory a certain number of senators (a quorum that is fifty-one after a vote), must be present for the Senate to conduct its business. You may often see the Senate in a "quorum call" during the day. This process is literally the clerk calling senators' names at a very slow pace (with several-minute intervals between names). This is he or she calling the roll, assessing if there is a quorum present. This process, a "quorum call," is often used for purposes other than actually calling the roll. A quorum is usually not present at all times, but, for example, often a senator appears to speak on the floor and end the quorum call before the clerk finishes the attendance list. The intent is usually to pause floor action in between speakers or activities and helps the bill managers or leaders control the floor, because the quorum call can only be called off by unanimous

yeas and nays requested and granted, and then the vote
will begin. The resulting vote brings a quorum to the
floor, ending the previous quorum call. That vote is
often used to create focus and have conversations to
help move business forward and is subject to a majority threshold. The threshold for what counts as "absent
quorum" depends on the floor situation. The calling of
the quorum that precedes a vote—where the clerk calls
the names of senators and discovers that a quorum is
not present—depends on what is happening on the
floor. After a vote, the clerk will assume that a majority should be present.

Motion to appeal the ruling of the chair   This is a way
of attempting to overturn the chair's ruling on a particular issue. It is sometimes used to change precedent
(called "going nuclear"), change the rules of the Senate,
or to show some protest against a decision of the chair.
Sometimes it is used as a secondary protest against other
things happening on the floor. The actual vote format can
be a tabling vote of the motion to appeal or sustain the
ruling. To adopt a rules change by negotiation, not by the
"nuclear" mechanism, requires sixty-seven votes (two-
thirds of the Senate).

Motion to sustain a veto   If the president vetoes a
bill, it first returns to the chamber that originated it
("S" bill from the Senate or an "HR" bill from the
House). In the Senate, whether the Senate is first voting
to sustain a veto or has received the veto papers from the
House, the motion is subject to a threshold of two-
thirds of the Senate (thus it takes sixty-seven votes to
override a veto).

consent (which is usually granted) or by a vote. ,
issue is still being negotiated or a bill being consid(
to which managers don't want a troubling amendm
to be offered, they may hold the Senate in quorum c.
until there is a solution or settlement. It is often used t
protect the floor while awaiting the next senator to arrive to speak, used between Senate speakers so that debate time is "burning equally" between both parties or
opponents and proponents on a matter if there is limited
debate on both sides. Floor debate is structured either
informally through understandings between the cloakrooms or more formally with time agreements. This way,
the parties can plan when their members come to the
floor to speak and in those cases, it may matter greatly if
and how the non-speaking time on the floor is being
counted.

In some cases, a roll call vote is needed to exit the
quorum call. The shorthand "live quorum vote" is often
a good empty vessel vote, meaning it can offer use beyond the actual attainment of a quorum on the floor.
A vote may be needed to get members to the floor to
help talk or break an impasse; a senator may want to
slow things down, and so he or she objects to waiving
a quorum call or to coming out of the quorum call
quickly. Or a vote may be needed and nothing else is
available, so a quorum call is used. Again, look at the
context to see why a procedural move is happening.
When a live quorum happens, the clerk will call the roll
at a normal pace (as you might hear in school), find that
a quorum is not present, and inform the chair, which
he or she will announce. This calls for a motion to instruct the sergeant-at-arms to request the presence of
absent senators, the motion to instruct is made, the

Conference motions   Going to conference is a motion with three moves in one called a "compound motion": insisting on the Senate version of a bill or disagreeing to the House amendment, requesting the conference or agreeing to the House request for a conference, and authorizing the chair to appoint conferees while setting the conferee ratio. Members of the conference committee are usually selected from the members of the committee of jurisdiction of the bill being considered, but those selections are made at the discretion of the leaderships, so there is some gamesmanship involved. There is a compound motion to go to conference in the modern Senate that is subject to a single cloture vote if there is not cooperation—which means a 3/5 vote for cloture and up to two hours of debate. This is different from when a conference report comes back to the Senate, in which case it is privileged so is subject to just one cloture vote (three-fifths threshold), but then up to thirty hours of post-cloture debate.

Motion to instruct conferees   Before a bill goes to conference, the Senate can sometimes make a motion to advise the conferees on certain issues in a nonbinding way. Motions to instruct are often made as part of the compound motion to go to conference, post-cloture, and thus subject to a majority threshold of those present and voting. If it is made not in post-cloture conditions, it can be filibustered but the cloture is subject to abbreviated rules for going to conference (as noted above with the compound motion and two hours of debate).

Motion to waive   Generally a motion to waive is made in the context of waiving the Budget Act when a

provision in a bill violates the set budget caps in a given
fiscal year, or if there is some other violation of the Budget Act involved. Reconciliation bills need to comply
with several aspects of the Budget Act, one of which is
the Byrd Rule, for example. The threshold for waiving is
three-fifths.

Motion to reconsider   When someone wants to reconsider a previously failed vote, it takes three votes to
make that reconsideration. A motion to proceed to the
motion to reconsider the previously failed vote requires
a majority vote, the motion to reconsider the previously
failed vote requires a majority, and then the vote in question occurs again (at its original threshold, so if it was a
cloture vote on legislation, the threshold would be three-
fifths of the Senate).

Up-or-down vote   When someone refers to an up-
or-down vote, usually this means the vote is a majority
threshold, or that it was a vote set directly on an item at
any threshold (such as sixty) but without other procedural
votes needed. This can happen by consent pre-cloture on
an amendment, for example, or the amendment may be
set at sixty if it is controversial or non-germane as a way of
making its adoption more difficult. Up-or-down voting
can also happen post-cloture if there are germane amendments pending; they are subject to majority vote. Nominations can also be set at majority up-or-down votes with
agreement. It is often used as shorthand to mean "not cloture" but a vote just on the actual issue at hand.

Motion to concur   When the House sends a "message," a bill the Senate has already passed and the

House has further amended and sent back to the Senate, the Senate can move to concur (to agree with) the House amendment and pass the bill. The motion to concur is debatable, so if cloture is needed, there is a three-fifths threshold. If cloture is invoked (or cloture is not needed), the motion to concur itself is a majority vote. The Senate can also move to concur in the House amendment with a further amendment and send that back to the House, or the Senate can table the House amendment and return the vehicle to the House in its original form.

Cloture   Already discussed at length, cloture is designed to bring focus to the floor process on an issue and truncate debate. The motion to invoke cloture on a motion to proceed or to end debate on legislative items, or on an amendment, is subject to a three-fifths threshold. In the case of nominations, motions to invoke cloture on any nominations are subject to a majority threshold.

Nominations   With cooperation for consideration of a nomination, the nomination can be confirmed by voice vote or consent, or by timing the vote and setting an up/down vote at a certain time. But absent cooperation around consideration of the nomination, cloture is needed (majority threshold for all nominations). If debate is ended on any nomination, the confirmation vote itself is subject to a majority vote.

Treaties   While they are rarely seen on the floor, in addition to nominations, treaties are the other special calling of the Senate versus the House. Treaties are reviewed and ratified (or not, if there are not the votes) by the Senate. If there is cooperation this can happen by

consent, voice or division vote, or with time agreement;
without cooperation, treaties are subject to a two-thirds
of the Senate threshold for ratification and are debatable. Note that treaties are generally ratified with the
adoption of a "resolution of ratification" that includes
notes (not to the treaties themselves) that the senators
have added to their understanding of the reading and
application of the treaty.

"Extra votes"   In times of controversy, for example,
if a nominee is particularly contentious, the Senate
sometimes allows some of the behind the scenes action
to be on display. That means, occasionally, there are unusual or "extra votes." In these cases, votes are generally
majority thresholds so their outcome is known, and the
votes do not go to the heart of whatever matter is at
hand, so they are generally agreed to by consent or
voice vote and do not need a roll call vote. When a roll
call vote is required on one of these types of votes, it is
a sign that some senators are attempting to show great
protest or to delay action on a matter. For example, the
mandatory quorum call before a cloture vote, which is
usually waived by consent, can be required to have a
roll call vote. Another example is moving in and out of
Executive Session to consider specific nominations:
sometimes the majority will have to vote their way
into Executive Session and back out into legislative
session. This is unusual. So many possible maneuvers,
motions, and votes can be seen every so often for the
dedicated Senate watcher. When they occur, the question is what else is happening to bring this unusual
maneuver about, and the answer is usually something
very political.

Statutory vehicles Some vehicles operate outside the scope of the usual procedural mechanisms. For example, the vehicle that allowed for congressional review of the Iran nuclear deal was a special vehicle created by statute. Waivers for nominations are also sometimes structured in a specific way by statute. The more commonly used statutory vehicle is the Congressional Review Act, which created resolutions of disapproval—a means by which Congress can overturn recent administrative regulations (and prevent agencies from promulgating substantially similar rules until Congress acts again). They are very powerful, and have truncated Senate procedures. The motion to proceed to a resolution of disapproval is subject to a majority vote, and then the resolution itself is subject to up to ten hours of debate equally divided between opponents and proponents, and then an adoption vote at a majority threshold. It is not debatable (no cloture) and not amendable on the floor. The resolutions can be vetoed.

To Review, In Short

Following are the votes needed to move legislation forward.

Cloture on legislation—three-fifths (sixty votes)

Adoption or passage on legislation—majority

Cloture on nominations—majority

Confirmation on any nomination—majority

Tabling vote—majority

Cloture on motion to proceed when needed (this cloture not needed on privileged vehicles)—three-fifths (sixty)

Adoption of motion to proceed—majority

Cloture on conference or messages—three-fifths (sixty)

Adoption of conference report or motion to concur (passage of message)—majority

Treaty ratification—two-thirds (sixty-seven)

Veto override—two-thirds (sixty-seven)

Adoption of resolution of disapproval—majority

Fast-Moving or Unusual Vehicles

As mentioned earlier, the two main ways to move things forward are cloture and consent. A few additional special procedures can move a bill along faster than average.

Conference report   When the House and Senate have both passed their own versions of a bill in the same vehicle, one of the chambers may agree to the other chamber's version. If each chamber insists on pushing its own version, the chambers may agree to go to conference in a special conference committee to negotiate the differences and come up with one bill. The conference may be open to the public, but generally most of the negotiations occur behind the scenes. If the negotiations are successful, the conference committee produces a conference report, and this report is privileged, meaning that it can move relatively fast. Typically, a conference

report is first sent out to the chamber that controls the vehicle. Thus, an S bill goes to the Senate first, whereas an HR bill goes to the House first. Should the first chamber adopt the conference report without changes, it travels to the second chamber for consideration. In the Senate, the conference report is considered privileged, just like a message (see the next item), so the motion to proceed is also not debatable and can be moved on quickly with a simple majority vote. Thus, only one cloture is needed to pass a conference report.

If the Senate receives the conference report first, there are several points of order available, such as scope of the conference violations or to recommit the conference report to the conference committee for amendment. If the Senate receives the conference report from the House, there are still points of order available, but not the motion to recommit for the purpose of amendment. Basically, it is more difficult to change the conference report when it arrives in the Senate from the House, both procedurally and, generally, politically.

Messaging   Instead of going to formal conference, sometimes the chambers will ping-pong a bill back and forth until a consensus bill emerges. This is called "messaging." For example, the Senate may send a bill to the House, and the House may add an amendment and send it back to the Senate. The Senate has received a message from the House, and there is no need to debate the motion to proceed to that bill again. The House message relative to that Senate bill can be brought up by simple majority motion to proceed, and thus needs only one cloture on the motion to concur with the House message, which is like a vote to pass the bill. Note that this is fast by Senate standards but is not considered fast generally. A single cloture filing can still take three and one-half to four days, depending on the level of coop-eration. But it is still much faster than having to process cloture on a motion to proceed first.

Resolution of disapproval The Congressional Re-view Act created a powerful tool called a resolution of disapproval that can be introduced anytime, but, in order to enjoy the special procedures, it must be intro-duced within sixty days after the promulgation of a final rule. A resolution of disapproval can move through committee by petition after twenty days; on the floor it is privileged in that it can be moved with a simple ma-jority vote (not debatable, no cloture) and is subject to up to ten hours of debate equally divided between pro-ponents and opponents, and then a simple majority adoption vote (passage). Resolutions of disapproval are subject to veto like other vehicles, and that is often when they are defeated. They are powerful not only because of the special procedural powers, but also because if a reso-lution of disapproval is successful and a veto overturned or not made, then a given agency cannot promulgate a substantially similar regulation unless Congress acts again. Resolutions of disapproval are most successful in the period of transition between administrations, when an outgoing president's regulations may be disapproved and not protected by the new administration. The wide use of this tool is something seen only recently.

Budget resolutions, reconciliation, and the vote-a-rama Budget resolutions are often used by the majority party to express its priorities and as a means to create reconciliation instructions. This is notable in the Senate because it can be a rare means of moving legislative items that have budgetary impact with a majority vote, instead of a sixty-vote threshold usually needed with legislation. The budget resolution is subject to up to fifty hours of debate. After this a so-called vote-a-rama takes place during which amendments can be considered—or motions relative to those amendments such as to table or waive points of order—until all 100 senators decide they have finished offering amendments. At this point the Senate can vote on the resolution at a majority threshold. The vote-a-rama often serves as a time to test votes and message amendments, in addition to other substantive issues, as it is a chance for any member to offer something they want considered. This is in contrast to the difficulties in having amendments considered during the normal legislative process when a senator must gain access to a slot, navigate the floor managers, and often may need consent to have a vote. But in the vote-a-rama, the restrictions are far less, often based on the energy level of members, political factors, or peer pressure, but not procedural limitations.

If reconciliation instructions are included in a successful budget resolution, some committees may be instructed to follow those instructions and produce legislation. Reconciliation bills must be drafted in very specific ways, but if brought to the floor, they are subject to up to twenty hours of debate prior to a vote-a-rama.

Vote-a-ramas are a special time in the Senate, because usually a member must gain a slot on the amendment tree to get a vote on an amendment. Each step can have its own complications. Having an amendment considered on the floor is not guaranteed for any member. It often depends on context, timing, and cooperation levels on the floor. If the leader has filled the amendment tree—filled the available slots a bill starts with—it can be difficult to have an amendment offered absent a political fight. Or there may be slots available but a member opposes the amendment and won't grant consent to allow it to be made pending in a new slot. Or a member may get it pending but may not get consent to allow a vote. In that case, the amendment's being germane can help, as it will mean the member can get a vote post-cloture if cloture on the bill has been invoked.

The flow of an amendment tree will often depend on political context as much as procedural know-how. There may be an open slot, but will offering an amendment hurt the bill? Will the floor managers oppose it or support it? If the language is changed a little bit, can the floor managers adopt it by consent without risking a floor fight? Is there a reason to file the amendment but not offer it? Is there a negotiation unrelated to the bill expected? These are just some of the potential questions involved when considering amendments or evaluating why an amendment may have been filed or offered.

CHANGES IN THE SENATE RULES

With every new Congress, there are debates as to whether the Senate will change any of its rules and precedents. Some Congresses have seen changes, resulting from both cooperation and "nuclear" moves, and some have seen a full Congress go by without changes. As you follow a new Congress in the press, you may spot reports mentioning debates about the cloture threshold for motions to proceed, or even legislation. You may read about other floor maneuvers that some may want to limit or further simplify, such as the post-cloture time on nominations (which for one Congress was reduced by negotiation). Discussions of changes in the Senate rules or precedents are ongoing and lively, often resulting from political conversations that can impact the floor directly. The reader may witness some of these maneuvers, and we will do our best to document them in future updates.

THE SENATE AS A WHOLE

The life cycle of an idea or a bill in the Senate could be called a slow burn, in comparison to the potentially fast pace of the House (although even there it can take months or years to get some legislation moved forward). The Senate is a place of long memories, long relationships, and often long-term projects or campaigns for issues, a setting where one's word and ability to recognize what is possible in the moment matters greatly. Six-year terms offer a lot of time to get to know and work with other members, to build reputations, and to accumulate the kind of capital that comes from working with and helping others reach their goals as well. This means that although some bills may not be ready to move in the Senate during a particular Congress or year, an issue's momentum can build and legislation can be introduced over and over, until maybe several years and iterations later it is finally ripe for passage. Many of the largest legislative fights took the form of multiyear, multi-Congress discussions.

The slower burn of the Senate is also manifested in other ways. Senators may have more individual power than House members, in terms of their ability to make motions on the floor that can impact the pace of progress. But there are other tools as well. They, like House members, can also write letters to administration officials, business leaders, committee leaders, or others; introduce legislation; introduce amendments; convene meetings; hold hearings; ask questions at committee events; call press conferences; and more. It is a broad toolbox.

One of the ways voting and pressures differ between the two chambers is that senators, representing a whole state, may have a more diverse set of constituents, interests, businesses, localities, cities and rural areas, and pressures to consider than House members. Also, a full state cannot be gerrymandered in the same way some House districts can be, so the diverse constituencies remain intact year after year. This means that serious legislation (intended to move through both chambers) should generally be inclusive and broad enough to be considered acceptable to both large constituencies and representatives' districts. To compound the difficulty of crafting viable legislation that can survive the pressures in both chambers, it takes deals being cut to get the consent of 100 senators or the votes of sixty senators, and also the support of at least a majority in the House (or more if a bill is intended for the suspension calendar). It can be even more difficult to reach the sixty-vote cloture threshold needed to end debate if you do not have at least the timing cooperation of all members. If there is a negotiated cloture agreement, those opposed must make a judgment call as to how deeply they oppose the legislation. In some cases, even if they do not oppose the substance, there might be an opportunity to raise another important issue. This scenario often crosses party lines and can be driven more by subject matter or geography than politics. Senators must make a number of political calculations as they judge how to deal with matters moving through the floor or hotline/negotiations process. In the Senate, decisions about engaging in negotiations on, obstruction of, or support for legislative vehicles or nominations must be taken in that long-run context of what is done today may impact members' ability to make deals with their colleagues in the future, or may help garner promises for future action. For example, a bill may fail to get cloture on the first try, but then a negotiation happens over future action on an important matter that some members wanted to consider on the pending bill. Once the deal is made for future movement, a second attempt at cloture on the pending bill is successful. If a senator can convince enough colleagues to help him or her, this is another possible tool available to advocate for an issue.

FOUR

Conclusion

The United States Congress is an institution with two distinctly different bodies, each of which functions according to its own priorities, pressures, customs, and rules. This bicameral design creates contradiction in our federal legislative process, leading to periodic tension. Where the House's majority rule often responds to the immediate visceral concerns of the country's citizens hailing from the majority's party, grouped as they are in smaller districts, the Senate's larger, more diverse constituencies tend to produce deliberate moderation among a smaller number of legislators, with less power afforded to the majority party. From these different circumstances and dynamics is born the fundamental principle of balance in our federal government.

Trying to grasp the workings of Congress can lead to frustration. But it is important to bear in mind that the two chambers were designed to operate differently and often not in agreement or in sync—representative of a big country with vast interests. In short, the job of the legislative branch was meant to be hard. Ideas take time to develop, as do coalitions. While voluminous legislative production may be the hallmark of one Congress, gridlock can often define the next.

Senators and representatives have many tools to employ in speeding up or slowing down the process.

These include, but are not limited to, drafting bill and amendment language, delivering speeches on the Senate and House floors, and offering (or blocking) procedural motions. All of these tools can be enhanced and complemented with press-related and coalition-building strategies to broadcast a message or galvanize opinion outside the halls of Congress.

We hope this brief volume has helped readers gain a sense of admiration for the Congress, commensurate with our own love for the legislative branch. Members and their staff travel every district and every state as they address the issues of the day—Social Security or immigration or veterans' affairs—pushing to relay ideas from the local to national stage and back again, and shining a watchful light on the nation's concerns. It is not the flash you see on TV that counts. Every day in Congress the steady hum of work, meetings, advocacy, and planning occurs at a relentless pace. That's what makes the difference and we hope you see it too.

APPENDIX A

Sample House Weekly Schedule

KEVIN 🐻★ McCARTHY

MAJORITY LEADER

LEADER'S WEEKLY SCHEDULE

Week of April 3rd, 2016

MONDAY, APRIL 3RD
On Monday, the House will meet at 12:00 p.m. for morning hour and 2:00 p.m. for legislative business. Votes will be postponed until 6:30 p.m.

Legislation Considered Under Suspension of the Rules:

1) H.R. 479 - North Korea State Sponsor of Terrorism Designation Act of 2017, as amended *(Sponsored by Rep. Ted Poe / Foreign Affairs Committee)*

2) H.Res. 92 - Condemning North Korea's development of multiple intercontinental ballistic missiles, and for other purposes, as amended *(Sponsored by Rep. Joe Wilson / Foreign Affairs Committee)*

3) H.Res. 54 - Reaffirming the United States-Argentina partnership and recognizing Argentina's economic reforms, as amended *(Sponsored by Rep. Albio Sires / Foreign Affairs Committee)*

TUESDAY, APRIL 4TH
On Tuesday, the House will meet at 10:00 a.m. for morning hour and 12:00 p.m. for legislative business.

Legislation Considered Under Suspension of the Rules:

1) Concurring in the Senate Amendment to H.R. 353 - Weather Research and Forecasting Innovation Act of 2017 *(Sponsored by Rep. Frank Lucas / Science, Space, and Technology Committee)*

H.R. 1343 - Encouraging Employee Ownership Act of 2017, Rules Committee Print (Subject to a Rule) *(Sponsored by Rep. Randy Hultgren / Financial Services Committee)*

WEDNESDAY, APRIL 5TH
On Wednesday, the House will meet at 10:00 a.m. for morning hour and 12:00 p.m. for legislative business.

Legislation Considered Under Suspension of the Rules:

1) H.R. 1667 - Financial Institution Bankruptcy Act of 2017, as amended *(Sponsored by Rep. Tom Marino / Judiciary Committee)*

2) S. 544 - To amend the Veterans Access, Choice, and Accountability Act of 2014 to modify the termination date for the Veterans Choice Program, and for other purposes. *(Sponsored by Sen. Jon Tester / Veterans Affairs Committee)*

H.R. 1304 - Self-Insurance Protection Act (Subject to a Rule) *(Sponsored by Rep. Phil Roe / Energy and Commerce Committee)*

THURSDAY, APRIL 6TH
On Thursday, the House will meet at 9:00 a.m. for legislative business. Last votes expected no later than 3:00 p.m.

H.R. 1219 - Supporting America's Innovators Act of 2017, Rules Committee Print (Subject to a Rule) *(Sponsored by Rep. Patrick McHenry / Financial Services Committee)*

MAJORITY LEADER'S FLOOR OFFICE • H-107 THE CAPITOL

Source: http://floor.majorityleader.gov/week-2017-04-02.pdf

APPENDIX B

Sample House Rules Committee Structured Rule

115th Congress
1st Session

H. Res. __

————

H.R. 1343 - Encouraging Employee Ownership Act of 2017

1. Structured rule.

2. Provides one hour of debate equally divided and controlled by the chair and ranking minority member of the Committee on Financial Services.

3. Waives all points of order against consideration of the bill.

4. Provides that an amendment in the nature of a substitute consisting of the text of Rules Committee Print 115-11 shall be considered as adopted and the bill, as amended, shall be considered as read.

5. Waives all points of order against provisions in the bill, as amended.

6. Makes in order only the further amendment printed in the Rules Committee report, if offered by the Member designated in the report, which shall be considered as read, shall be debatable for the time specified in the report equally divided and controlled by the proponent and an opponent, shall not be subject to amendment, and shall not be subject to a demand for division of the question.

7. Waives all points of order against the amendment printed in the report.

8. Provides one motion to recommit with or without instructions.

(continued)

Appendix B

RESOLUTION

Resolved, That upon adoption of this resolution it shall be in order to consider in the House the bill (H.R. 1343) to direct the Securities and Exchange Commission to revise its rules so as to increase the threshold amount for requiring issuers to provide certain disclosures relating to compensatory benefit plans. All points of order against consideration of the bill are waived. An amendment in the nature of a substitute consisting of the text of Rules Committee Print 115-11 shall be considered as adopted. The bill, as amended, shall be considered as read. All points of order against provisions in the bill, as amended, are waived. The previous question shall be considered as ordered on the bill, as amended, and on any further amendment thereto, to final passage without intervening motion except: (1) one hour of debate equally divided and controlled by the chair and ranking minority member of the Committee on Financial Services; (2) the further amendment printed in the report of the Committee on Rules accompanying this resolution, if offered by the Member designated in the report, which shall be in order without intervention of any point of order, shall be considered as read, shall be separately debatable for the time specified in the report equally divided and controlled by the proponent and an opponent, and shall not be subject to a demand for a division of the question; and (3) one motion to recommit with or without instructions.

SUMMARY OF AMENDMENT PROPOSED TO BE MADE IN ORDER
(summaries derived from information provided by sponsors)

Sponsor	#	Description	Debate Time
1. Polis (CO)	#2	Requires GAO to report to Congress one year after date of enactment the impact of the legislation on employee ownership.	(10 minutes)

Source: https://rules.house.gov/sites/republicans.rules.house.gov /files/Rule-%20HR%201343.pdf

APPENDIX C

Sample Senate Hotline Email

SUBJECT: HOTLINE - S. RES. 714 - A RESOLUTION STATING THERE ARE SEVEN DAYS IN A WEEK

The Majority Leader asks unanimous consent that the Senate proceed to the consideration of S. Res. 714, submitted by Senator XYZ and others.

The Majority Leader then asks consent that the resolution be agreed to, and the preamble be agreed to.

S. Res. 714 - Resolution recognizing that there are seven days in a week.

If your Senator has any objections, please call the Cloakroom.

APPENDIX D

Samples of Most Common Amendment Trees

Unemployment Compensation Extension Act of 2009 (H.R. 3548)—"Substitute Tree"

- Reid-Baucus amendment in the nature of a substitute (#2712)

  - Reid first-degree amendment to Baucus-Reid substitute amendment #2712, to change the enactment date (#2713)

    - Reid second-degree amendment to Reid amendment #2713, of a perfecting nature (#2714)

- Reid amendment to the language proposed to be stricken by Baucus-Reid substitute amendment #2712, to change the enactment date (#2715)

  - Reid amendment to Reid amendment #2715, of a perfecting nature (#2716)

- Reid amendment to the motion to recommit to change the enactment date (#2717)

  - Reid first-degree amendment to Reid amendment #2717, of a perfecting nature (#2718)

- Reid second-degree amendment to Reid amendment #2718, of a perfecting nature (#2719)

H.R. 5325 (legislative vehicle for a short-term continuing resolution 2016)—"Substitute Tree"

- Cochran amendment in the nature of substitute (#5082) [text of the short-term CR]

  - McConnell amendment to change the enactment date. (#5083)

    - McConnell second-degree amendment to McConnell amendment #5083, of a perfecting nature. (#5084)

- McConnell amendment to the language proposed to be stricken by Cochran substitute amendment #5082, to change the enactment date. (#5085)

  - McConnell second-degree amendment to McConnell amendment #5085, of a perfecting nature. (#5086)

- McConnell motion to commit H.R. 5325 to the Appropriations Committee with instructions to report back forthwith with an amendment to change the enactment date (#5087).

  - McConnell amendment to the instructions of the McConnell motion to commit, of a perfecting nature. (#5088)

    - McConnell second-degree amendment to McConnell amendment #5088, of a perfecting nature. (#5089)